all in.

EXPLORING WHAT IT MEANS TO BE ALL IN THE GOSPEL OF JESUS CHRIST

all in.

EXPLORING WHAT IT MEANS TO BE
ALL IN THE GOSPEL OF JESUS CHRIST

Morgan Jones

MORGAN JONES, GENERAL EDITOR

DESERET
BOOK

SALT LAKE CITY, UTAH

Opposite page: Ryan Smith, "Be All In," *Marriott School Alumni Magazine* (Fall 2019).

IMAGE CREDITS: All photos used by permission. *Deseret News*/Kristin Murphy: pages vi, 40, 62. Getty Images: page viii. Kensie Smith: pages 2, 43, 51. Busath Photography: page 4. *Deseret News*/Eric Betts: page 6. Derek Campbell: page 13. Daniel Steiner: page 20. Time Out for Women/Macy Robison: page 22, 145. *Deseret News*/ Jeffrey Allred: pages 23, 82, 127, 128, 149, 154. Tell the Birds/Breea Bringham: pages 24, 88. Colin Rivera: page 26. Lola Ogunbote: page 30. Lindsay Ricks: page 31. *Deseret News*/Ravell Call: pages 32, 54, 61, 83, 135, 150. *LDS Living*/Jed Wells: page 41, 100, 122. Getty Images/Mike Coppola: page 44. Deseret Book/ Jasmine Mullen: pages 47, 75, 116, 125. Getty Images/George Frey: page 48. Laurel Christensen Day: page 59. Matthew Imbler: page 60. *Deseret News*/Scott G. Winterton: pages 65, 95. Pack Photo & Video: page 76. Jess Kettle: pages 79, 162. Jensen Sutta: page 97. Hal Boyd: page 98. Time Out for Women: pages 102, 112. *Deseret News*/Spenser Heaps: pages 103, 110. Morgan Jones: page 104. *Deseret News*/Adam Fondren: page 108. Jacob Hess: page 126. *Deseret News*/Hans Koepsell: page 138. BYUtv: page 143.

Library of Congress Cataloging-in-Publication Data

(CIP data on file)
ISBN 978-1-62972-918-3

Printed in the United States of America
PubLitho, Draper, UT

10   9   8   7   6   5   4   3   2   1

Being all in is the lost art of really committing to something. Real commitment is hard. Technology and social media have raised our awareness and we live in a constant state of FOMO (fear of missing out).

We live in the ultimate on-demand world—where there's always a backup plan, where there's always an off-ramp, and where commitment feels binding to a lot of people.

I am here to testify that the only way to feel successful in life is to make decisions wisely, and then act on those decisions with 100% commitment.

—RYAN SMITH, QUALTRICS CEO AND UTAH JAZZ OWNER

A Note to Readers

If you have been a faithful listener of the *All In* podcast, I'm thrilled you're reading this book.

This book is my thank you to you. I truly believe time is valuable. Each second, each breath is a gift from God, and I am glad you have found this podcast to be worth your investment. It is my greatest hope that you will find this book to be worth it as well.

If you have never heard of the *All In* podcast, I'm thrilled you're reading this book.

I'm your host, Morgan Jones, and I'll be guiding you through this book. All you really need to know before we get started is that at the end of each episode of the podcast, we ask one final question: "What does it mean to you to be 'all in' the gospel of Jesus Christ?"

If you're like me, you'll come into this book with your own ideas of what being "all in" means. I'd like to invite you to consider your own answer to this question and then set that answer aside during our time together. In the end, I hope you'll see that your answer has changed—at least a little bit. I hope you'll find there is no one way to be all in.

Introduction

___

I want to invite you into a room. It's not much to see. One wall in the room is painted green. It was originally intended to serve as a green screen for video projects but was never actually utilized as such. Another wall is covered by a whiteboard that someone forgot to erase, thus becoming an eyesore. This room is the closest thing we had to a studio for the first year and a half of the podcast. I was always kind of embarrassed to bring people into the room, and if I were walking you from the elevator, I would likely make a joke so its appearance wasn't a complete letdown. But that's the funny thing about sacred spaces—the Spirit can quietly transform even the most unlikely place into something special, sometimes so subtly that we don't even realize it, until one day you walk out of that space for the last time and have to walk back in just once more to remember what you experienced there.

For me, this room in the back corner of the third floor of the old Deseret Book office building has become a sacred space. It is a place where I had conversations I'm well aware I never would've had otherwise. I once heard a saying: "Go deep fast."[1] And if there's anything this  podcast has allowed me to do, it is to cut the small talk and skip straight to the stuff that really matters. In this room, I had conversations about race, Church history, divorce, excommunication, abuse, death, and cancer. And in at least one case, it would be impossible—at least in this life—to have the conversation again.

You've likely had moments in your own life when you felt like you needed to pinch yourself. For me, just about any time I sit in this room, I feel like I need to pinch myself. You see, I grew up reading Church magazines, Deseret Book publications, the *Church News*, and pretty much anything Church-related I could get my hands on. My motivation was pretty simple: I just wanted to feel connected

1. Morgan Jones, "How Greg Madsen Taught Me How to Live after He Died," *Deseret News*, September 12, 2017.

to my faith. As a teenager, I attended Time Out for Women with my mama and bought a book by Jane Clayson Johnson. The book was called *I Am a Mother*, and I wish I could tell you why I read it as a fifteen-year-old. What I can tell you is that the second chapter of that book is an absolute masterpiece. In it, Johnson tells her story of arriving at Brigham Young University. "I had a very detailed outline, a precise timeline, for myself—and for the Lord! The wedding colors were set (peach and teal). My dress was picked out (McCall's pattern #7847). And I'd compiled a list of baby names (Lauren, Sydney, or Elizabeth for a girl, Matthew, Ryan, or David for a boy)."[2] But she then explains how her life ended up taking a very different trajectory than the one she'd imagined. And from the first time I read it, I had a distinct feeling my life was not going to follow the path I had imagined. I've never picked out

> I AM LIKE A LITTLE PENCIL IN [GOD'S] HAND.
>
> Mother Teresa

my wedding dress pattern, but I do have a solid list of baby names I've been sitting on for a good decade. That chapter in Jane's book also included a statement by Mother Teresa that became my favorite quote ever: "I am like a little pencil in [God's] hand. That is all.

---

2. Jane Clayson Johnson, *I Am a Mother* (Salt Lake City: Deseret Book, 2007), 44.

He does the thinking. He does the writing. The pencil has nothing to do with it. The pencil has only to be allowed to be used."[3]

In her case, Jane Clayson Johnson went on to be a much bigger deal than I will ever be, reporting on *Good Morning America* and working as a co-anchor on *The Early Show*. But I will say that the opportunities God has given me have surpassed my wildest expectations. I consistently feel inadequate and underqualified to sit at this table as I interview people who are much wiser than I will ever be. I am learning that the Lord enables us to do things we would be incapable of doing on our own. I am learning He allows us to sit at tables we may not necessarily belong at because there is something we can gain from that experience.

In her book, Johnson tells of a blessing she received from Elder Neal A. Maxwell as she prepared to appear on *The Early Show* for the first time. "You must allow the Lord to use you. . . . Sometimes

---

3. "Mother Teresa: Missionary of Compassion," *Time*, December 4, 1989.

you will not understand what He is doing . . . or why He is doing it. But do not question. You must allow Him to guide and direct you."[4]

For me, this has meant an exploration into what it means to be all in the gospel of Jesus Christ, and I'd like to invite you to come into this room with me. I hope you'll ignore the dry-erase marker permanently etched on the wall and instead focus on the person across the table from you. Look into their eyes and listen closely as they describe what it means to them to be all in. As you listen to their experiences and their perspectives, and as you have new experiences in your life, I hope that what

I HOPE THAT WHAT IT MEANS TO YOU TO BE ALL IN CHANGES AND EVOLVES

it means to you to be all in changes and evolves. It certainly has for me, and it'll happen again in the time that you and I spend together. You see, I think a big part of being all in is continually moving forward . . . further and further in.

So, make yourself comfortable and have a seat on the black faux-leather chair to the left. I'll record a full intro later, but for now, I'm just going to do the "This is *All In*" part, and then I'll welcome our guest and we'll roll. Are you ready? Let's do this.

---

4.   Jane Clayson Johnson, *I Am a Mother* (Salt Lake City: Deseret Book, 2007), 54.

CHAPTER ONE

All In,
One Day at a Time

——

"There's a place for you. There's a place for everyone.
We need you." —COURTNEY RICH

"Morgan, I don't know if I can do this."

My friend Bre Lasley was on the other end of the line and had called me in the middle of the workday.

I first met Bre on the second anniversary of the home intrusion that could've very easily taken her life. We were at a weekend retreat and were assigned to be roommates. Bre and I always tell people you bond very quickly when you're assigned to share a room with a complete stranger. The first night we stayed up until 3:00 a.m. talking and she told me her story. Just in case you missed her episode, let me briefly recap: Five years ago, Bre was getting ready for bed when she heard a man's voice outside her open window say, "Hey, girl. I'm coming in." The man climbed into Bre's bedroom, and for six minutes, she and her sister Kayli fought for their lives. Miraculously, a police officer happened to be in the neighborhood and heard cries for help. Kayli led him to the basement, where the intruder held a knife against Bre's throat—the same knife he had already used to stab her. The officer aimed and fired, killing the intruder and saving Bre's life. It was a miracle, and Bre has always given all the glory to God. In fact, in a video following the attack, Bre can be heard saying, "Heavenly Father was there the entire time, the entire time."

The story is nearly unbelievable, and Bre does an incredible job telling it, so I was thrilled when she agreed to do the podcast. We set a date and scheduled a time, and then she called. I could tell simply by the tone of her voice that she was stressed out. She explained to me that while she absolutely has a testimony of the gospel, there were things she had questions about and sometimes she didn't feel "all in." She didn't want to pretend to be something she was not. If I could've, I would've jumped through the phone right then and there, given her a hug, and told her that this is precisely why we needed her on this podcast.

I explained something to her that I want to make very clear

up front in this book: Our greatest hope with this podcast is to show that there are many ways to be all in the gospel of Jesus Christ—that when we speak of being "all in," it is not a reference to being either all in or all out. There is a lot of in-between.

THERE ARE MANY WAYS TO BE ALL IN THE GOSPEL OF JESUS CHRIST

So that day on the phone, I told Bre I wanted her to be totally honest with where she was in her faith. I assured her I would never want to misrepresent her faith either.

A week later, Bre sat across from me, and when I asked that final question, this was her answer:

"I love this question, and it was really thought-provoking, and I've been thinking about it ever since you asked me to come on the podcast. I think my best answer came [while] thinking about the sacrament prayers. Because I do struggle. There are things that I struggle with, and I think that it's okay to have questions. It's okay to have doubts, and you can be all in. This is what I'm learning, literally this week, that I can still be all in. I think I was so hard on myself—I felt like I couldn't even do this podcast, honestly. . . . But at the end of the day, I know that I have Heavenly Parents who love me, that gave me a Savior, that gave me an opportunity to live a wonderful life with a wonderful family, and a chance to live together forever. I think that for my answer of what it means to be all in, it is to be willing to be like Jesus, just like we try to every Sunday. I think it's being willing to take His name upon us, meaning just every day [being like], 'I just want to be more like Jesus.' And if I can take that promise literally, daily, then that's kind of my answer. [It] is just always remain willing."

In his October 2020 general conference talk, President Russell M. Nelson said, "The word *willing* is crucial to this interpretation of *Israel*. . . . We can choose to be of Israel, or not. We can choose to let God prevail in our lives, or not. We can choose to let God be the most powerful influence in our lives, or not."

When I look back, the people who have been on this podcast are not perfect, but they are willing, and they are honest about their faith. None of us know what we are going to go through tomorrow, or the next day, or the day after that, or how those experiences will affect or shape our beliefs. But what we do know is what we believe in an individual, isolated moment. In each interview, we talk with people in those very moments—these interviews represent just a small snapshot of their faith over the course of a lifetime. So, while beliefs could change with time for any one of the people in this book, I believe there is beauty in what they chose to share on that particular day during the time we spent together. That belief and their individual desire to share it publicly will be a part of their stories forever.

On our very first episode, speaking of looking back at history, Janiece Johnson, a historian at Brigham Young University, said, "I believe the real story is always better than the fake story. It often requires more work on our part. And we have to be willing to deal with the messiness. When you've got human beings who are full of opposition, it is always going to be messy. . . . When we're dealing with difficult topics, with human beings who are limited and mortal, there is going to be messiness. And I believe that if we approach the messiness head-on, there is strength and power in that. The gospel will still be true."

IT IS OUR MESS THAT ALLOWS US TO CONNECT WITH ONE ANOTHER

Don't you find that to be true of the present just as much as of the past? It is that messiness that we have tried to capture on this podcast, whether it be my mess or your mess or our guests' mess. It is my belief that it is our mess that allows us to connect with one another.

It is acknowledging that our faith is imperfect and that we have questions but then turning to God with those questions. And isn't that the essence of the gospel we believe in?

As Sister Sharon Eubank said in her answer to our final question, "I think about a fourteen-year-old boy who went into a grove because he had a question. And he emerged with this absolute confidence that Jesus Christ knew who he was and had a work for him to do. And we live in a world where Satan's had millennia to structure it in such a way that it distracts us so that we're half in or mostly out or all out. And for me, being all in means that I'll take my questions to Jesus Christ—He's the most important source for my questions—and that I have the confidence that He absolutely knows who I am, that He

> ## BEING ALL IN MEANS THAT I'LL TAKE MY QUESTIONS TO JESUS CHRIST
> Sister Sharon Eubank

has a work for me to do. Jesus Christ is the biggest, most powerful thing that's ever happened to me. It's His mercy and His love and His patience with me. I just love His gospel and I love His ways, and I want to tell everyone about this joy. He knows my name. He answers my questions. He forgives my mistakes. He wants my help. And that's what keeps me all in."

Church historian and author Patrick Mason communicated a similar thought: "I think too often in the Church, we have a spirit of fear. We are just afraid. We're afraid of the wheels coming off. We're afraid of somebody saying the wrong thing,  or thinking the wrong thing, or doing the wrong thing. We just have so much fear in the Church, and it's because the Church and the gospel are so precious to us. We don't want it to be damaged. We don't want our testimonies to be damaged. We don't want other people to be hurt. We have so much fear, but that is exactly the opposite of what Jesus teaches—what the Apostles taught. They said, 'Don't have a spirit of fear, have the spirit of love,' and so in this Church, we are not afraid of any question that can be thrown at us, because . . . this is the restored gospel of Jesus Christ. If it's true, then why would we be afraid of any question? We don't always have the answers, but we also have a ninth article of faith that says we can get the answers, and that there's more restoration coming. There's more revelation coming. But we have to ask the questions. Most of the sections of the Doctrine and Covenants came in answer [to] Joseph's questions. The First Vision came in answer to Joseph's question. The Restoration walks hand in hand with people [who] search for a greater light and knowledge. That is what the Restoration is—it's a restoration of truth to a world in confusion, a world with questions, and a world that doesn't know who God is—who Jesus is. And so this is the gift of the Restoration, [it] is that if you have questions, God will give answers."

So before we get too far into this book, I want you to know that no matter where you are at with your faith, there is a place for you in this Church and within the pages of this book. Writer McArthur Krishna said, "All in actually means all of us [are] welcome. . . . All of us as an entire humanity [are] welcome, but I also mean, on the micro-level, all of me is welcome. If I'm going to be all in, that means I bring my whole self. That means foibles, imperfections, stubbornness, feistiness, opinions, energy, laziness, and whatever else. Being all in means my Heavenly Parents and my brother Jesus always love me. And if you know that, it's easy. Well, it's not easy, but if you know that, then it's possible to be all in, because all of you is welcome."

The important thing is that you're willing, and if there is any little part of you that so much as "desires to believe" (see Alma 32:27), come on in. Come all in.

Camron Wright

NOVELIST

———

"I think maybe many would say that being all in means that we should be strong, valiant, and committed to the gospel, and I think perhaps it does mean that. But the problem, at least for me, is that I stumble. I make mistakes. I have days where I'm not strong, I'm not valiant, I'm not as committed as I should be. And I may even start to wonder if God's too busy for me—if He's really listening. And in fact, one of my favorite movie lines is in the film *Return to Me*, and it's this moment where an exasperated Minnie Driver looks heavenward, and she declares, 'What was God thinking?' I have those moments all the time, and I think that's okay. I can be human. I can still make mistakes, and yet I can be all in, if at the end of the day, I know where to look for redemption from those failings. I think if I remember to keep Christ at the center of my life in all that I do, if I try and cultivate a love for others, [even] if it's just a fraction of the love He has for me, then yeah, I may not be 'all in,' but I can certainly feel the sun on my face and I think I'm inching in the right direction. . . . That's what it represents to be all in."

McArthur Krishna

AUTHOR

——

"There's no time where it's not a good idea to turn to God. Whether or not you feel dirty, whether or not you feel wicked, whether or not you feel a failure, whether or not you feel irresponsible, whether or not you feel brain-exploding cognitive dissonance, it does not matter, whether or not you feel beautiful and pure and holy. All of those times, wherever you are, is the time to remember that you have Heavenly Parents who love you and to get—I was going to say get down on your knees, but it doesn't matter—curl up in a fetal position, whatever you need to do, to turn to God and say, 'Be with me.' I guess that's the success story in this. It's not the pinnacle, but the success story is the continued realization for the need to recommit and try again. This life is about trying again and trying again and trying again."

Eric Dyches

MENTAL HEALTH ADVOCATE

—

"I don't pretend to have it all figured out. For me . . . I would say if you are regularly thinking about the Savior and you have a genuine desire to treat His children—your brothers and sisters— well, and you want to develop those cardinal attributes; you want to be a forgiving person, you want to give to people, you want to show mercy, you want to have charity in your life and be seen as someone that has charity; if you think about the Savior and you think about Him regularly and you want to develop those attributes, I think you can check the box of being all in. . . . I know people that are listening right now, some people close to me, who've had some pretty major struggles in their life. . . . And if you ask them, 'Are you all in?' They would say, 'No, I'm not all in because of all these reasons why I'm not.' And in reality, I look at them and they are my inspirations. . . . So if you think regularly of the Savior, and you want to develop His attributes, I don't think I need to complicate it any more than saying, 'I'm all in and I'm going to keep going.'"

Emily Orton

HOMESCHOOLING MOM AND AUTHOR

"All of my questions and doubts have peace and rest not in being answered, but in knowing that the answer will ultimately present me with some new way that God is showing His love for me."

Olga Campora

AUTHOR, RAISED UNDER COMMUNIST
RULE IN CZECHOSLOVAKIA

———

"Don't be afraid to take an imperfect action.
. . . Many times, especially as members of The
Church of Jesus Christ of Latter-day Saints,
when we do something, we just want it to be
perfect. And I totally get that because all of us—
we strive with that. But I have learned through
my life how important it is not to be afraid to
take the imperfect action, because it is by doing
things that we really learn."

Chelsie Hightower

PROFESSIONAL DANCER

—

"I learned that His love is far different than I thought it was. In a very real sense—it doesn't matter how many times you've messed up or how far you fall, that love is always there."

Debra Theobald McClendon

LICENSED PSYCHOLOGIST

—

"The Atonement covers doubts, it covers our
fears, it covers even the things that we think
are so blasphemous. We condemn ourselves
for that; God does not condemn us for that.
As we turn to Him through the Atonement of
our Savior, He allows us, through the Savior, to
become whole, and He welcomes us home."

Wendy Ulrich

LICENSED PSYCHOLOGIST

"I mentioned that we are called the house of Israel, and that's a powerful name that means someone who has wrestled with God until God prevails, or until we prevail with God. It's not clear which way it goes from what I understand of the Hebrew word. But I am grateful that the Lord allows us to wrestle and invites us to wrestle with Him, and that He is willing to come and join us in the wrestle. And for me, part of what it means to be all in is to be willing to go to the Lord in honesty, when we are struggling with things, and to invite Him into the process, trusting fully—as fully as we can at any given moment—that He is fair, that He is all-knowing, that He is all-loving and kind, [and] that He absolutely has our best interests at heart. That He's not just withholding something from us out of meanness, spite, or judgment; but sometimes when He's holding something back, it's because the wrestle is part of our growth."

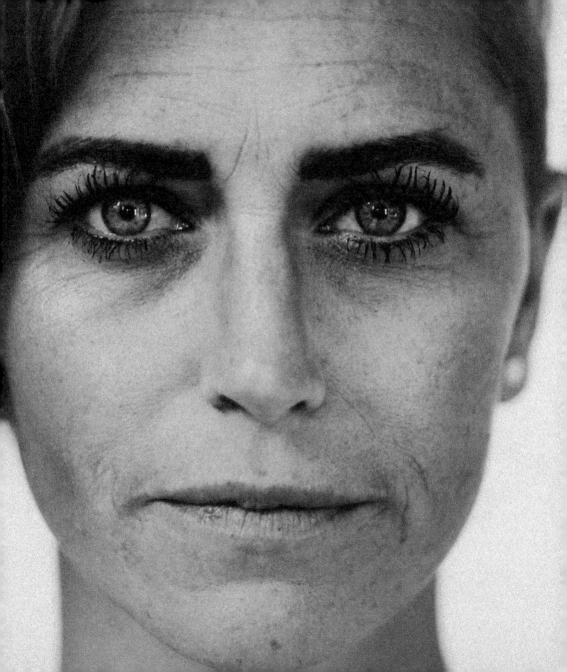

CHAPTER TWO

All In
Our Mortal Experience

——

Let me tell you about one of my favorite women we have ever had on *All In*.

Kim White is the kind of person who invites you over to her house for a game night just days after you interview her for the first time (true story). She never mentions the game you won again but is sure to bring up the game she beat you in at every subsequent opportunity. She even sends you a Marco Polo talking trash and challenging you to another game while recovering from surgery. You only have to meet Kim once for her to have a significant impact on your life. Actually . . . you don't have to meet Kim at all. You just had to follow her on her Instagram account, @kimcankickit, where she inspired thousands. You may have seen hashtags inspired by Kim's battle with cancer, which flooded social media toward the end of her life, including one that invited others to do something active and tag it #IDoItForKim. My personal all-time favorite post on the account was a video of Kim and her daughter lip syncing a song called "In My Blood," by Shawn Mendes, which spoke of not giving up. Despite Kim's headbanging with a huge smile on her face, I still can't watch that video without tearing up.

I guess I just always assumed, given the name of the Instagram account, that Kim believed she would beat cancer. So I was surprised when I interviewed her to hear her say that she felt like she would know when it was finally her time to go. She seemed to know it would be cancer that would take her life.

"I think that's such a blessing when you're diagnosed with any kind of disease, illness, or something that you think might take your life away, because you get woken up and you realize how precious life is, and you wish that you  didn't need something like that to really wake you up. But it definitely woke me up and I'm so thankful for that, because when they gave us two to three months to live, two other times, I just felt like in those moments . . . they were wrong. I was like, 'Nope, we're going to keep fighting, we're going to keep going,' you know? Who knows the day? I think I'll know when the doctors are actually right about my diagnosis. I just feel like I've been guided so well that I'll be like, 'Okay, this time, it's true. And this time they are right.'"

And when the time came, I cried all day. I wrote on Instagram: "My mom never met Kim but, like the tens of thousands of people who followed her online, she loved her." And that day, February 14, 2020, my mom sent a picture of some little baby shoes. I vaguely remembered Kim selling these shoes online, but my mom said, "I ordered these little shoes from Kim a while back to save for your little ones." I don't have kids, but I thought about how someday I'll put those shoes on a baby. When they outgrow those shoes, I'll put them in a treasure box. And when they are old enough to understand, I'll tell them about Kim and how I hope those shoes inspire them to live like her, breathing in every moment and appreciating the gift of every single day. I'll teach them that giving up isn't in our blood, and when they feel discouraged, I'll encourage them to keep fighting. I'll tell them to do it for Kim.

In her episode of the podcast, Jenny Reeder, a Church historian, said that in her study of history she can look back and see "how it all fits together, all these different little pieces, and so often in my own life, I'm stuck in this moment." And isn't this true of all of us?

As long as we're living, understanding what exactly is happening in our lives can be confusing. But when we look back, we see what Kim White said she saw in retrospect when she reflected on her battle with cancer:

"Experience shows you that you survived something, and then you can look back . . . and see the beauty. 'Oh, this happened and that's pretty amazing, God was still there. . . . Oh, look, He was still there, He's always been there.' I'm so grateful that I now can see it in the midst of it, the beauty in the darkness. We were studying the scriptures with our daughter just barely in the lesson about light and how much brighter it is when you are in a dark room. You turn on a flashlight in the light and it makes it a little brighter, but when you're in the dark, how drastic the difference is. And I think that's part of trials. [It's] that you appreciate the light so much more because you've experienced the darkness."

In her all-in answer, Emily Orton spoke of our commitment to and appreciation of our mortal experience and the importance of understanding that this is something we chose.

> I'M SO GRATEFUL THAT I NOW CAN SEE IT IN THE MIDST OF IT, THE BEAUTY IN THE DARKNESS.
>
> Kim White

"It wasn't just God sending me off, it was me sort of knocking at the gate, saying, 'I want to be like you, I want to see what I can do. . . . I think I'll be valiant, I think I'll be faithful. Give me a chance to know what a physical body really feels like, to get into some of these relationships, to find out what hunger is, to find out what it is to be tired, and know if I can still love other people under those circumstances.' We're in this total immersion experience, whether we realize it or not."

I think that Kim White also understood that life is messy, and I think that if we are to truly be all in this mortal experience, we have to understand that too. We signed up for this. We wanted this. And we never know how much time we have, so why not choose to be all in this one life—this one moment—right now?

Lola Ogunbote

SOCCER COACH AND ADVOCATE

"When we say we're all in, we say to God that 'I choose you. I choose you when things are going well. I choose you when things are hard. I choose you when I'm confused. I choose you when I'm hurt. I choose you when I'm disappointed. I choose you when I'm celebrating. I choose you when I'm blessed. I choose you when I feel joy. I choose you when life is going my way.' It's a beautiful affirmation. It's a beautiful strength. It's a beautiful way to use our

 agency to say to God, 'I'm in this with you, irrespective of what happens.' And that's a mindset that I've been trying to adopt. It's not been easy, but I really feel that when we say we're all in, we say to God that we choose Him. And we choose Him because obviously—He chose us first."

Lindsay Ricks

MOTHER OF A SON WITH DOWN SYNDROME

———

"I have an aunt that called me and said, 'Lindsay, I was thinking about you and William, and I had this little impression that I wanted to share with you.' And she said, 'I pictured the premortal life, and I felt like you knew William and you wanted him in your family, almost like you called dibs on him and you told everybody  to back off, that he was yours.' When she said that, I mean I still get emotional thinking about it, tears just welled up into my eyes, and I just felt like I chose this. This is not Heavenly Father doing something to hurt me. And I don't claim to understand how it all works, but for me and in my own experience, I feel like I chose to have William as part of my family. I feel like I did do that. I feel like I would do it now—'Everybody, he is mine. Back off. He's coming to my family.' That's just my personality. I understood there's a plan to this, there was a purpose. . . . so every time things have gotten hard and difficult and the unexpected has happened, I've just said to myself, 'I chose this and I wanted this for a reason.'"

CHAPTER THREE

All In
as a Single Adult

——

My first Sunday attending my neighborhood ward was in the middle of the COVID-19 pandemic. I walked in and an usher immediately asked me one question: "Are you here with a family?" When I said no, she directed me to a row of folding chairs against the back wall of the chapel where several other single sisters were sitting a safe distance from one another. We remained there for the duration of the meeting watching the families in front of us, seemingly from the outside looking in.

Now, I should say that my ward has been wonderful in the days and weeks since then, but a laundry list of experiences like this one has led me to try to give voice, when appropriate, to the challenges of single adults in the Church.

Still, I knew that if we tackled the topic on *All In*, we had to get it right. I had to do it justice, because the truth is, I would call being single into my thirties the most formative—even sacred—experience of my life up to this point. I had a couple of goals up front: (1) I wanted people to walk away with a clearer understanding of the challenges of being single in the Church. (2) I wanted to make sure it didn't feel like I was throwing a pity party and inviting people to join me.

As I was trying to think of someone who might be able to strike this delicate balance, I remembered a Sunday School lesson I had recently attended where Mallory Everton from the original cast of *Studio C* taught about Noah's Ark. I laughed, I got teary-eyed, and, in the end, I wrote a blog post inspired by her lesson. I knew she was the woman for the job.

Fortunately, Mallory graciously agreed. And despite the fact that we had never really met before, our interview felt like a solid replication of countless conversations I have had over the last five years of my life with dear friends over dinner, on hikes, on car rides, during phone calls, and on long walks.

"I think the most valuable thing that every individual can do is [be] very genuine and honest about your experience that you're having," she said on the episode. "Be genuine, say what's hard for you when you're talking, when you're sharing a comment, when you're teaching, or when you're speaking. Don't assume that everyone else is living an ideal and that they don't feel the way you feel. Just talk about your experience. I think you'll be shocked by how many people come up and feel just like you do. Even if you are single and they're married, or whatever, you'll discover those similarities between each other. And I think that's the greatest gift you can give every community you're in . . . your true and honest vulnerability."

It was that vulnerability she spoke of, cultivated by a very unique shared life situation, that allowed me and Mallory to immediately form a connection—the same vulnerability that has led to some of the most treasured friendships of my life. You see, one of the beauties of being a single adult is that you learn to take care of each other.

I'll never forget one day when I had a feeling that I needed to take a gift over to a friend in my stake who had recently gone through a breakup. The thought had come to me earlier in the week, and I even had a gift ready to take over, but I kept remembering at the most inconvenient times—right before bed or during the workday. By the time Sunday rolled around, I was beating myself up for not having taken the gift already when the thought came to me, "Take it now. Don't wait any longer." I went over and knocked on the door. At first, no one answered. I knocked again, and this time the door opened and there was my friend, who had clearly been crying. She said that very day would've been her and her ex-boyfriend's anniversary. In that moment, I knew why the thoughts earlier in the week had come at all the wrong times. I knew that God was aware of my friend and that He let me deliver a gift on His behalf, right on time.

I don't tell you this story to say, "Look at me, I'm so great," but because I literally cannot count the number of times I have been the person on the other side of that door; I could never count the angels that have visited me or sent a text or invited me on a trip. God has come to me in the form of some of my favorite things: Noosa yogurt, apple chips, acai bowls, fine chocolate bars, and the list goes on. That sounds crazy, but it's one hundred percent true.

But there are also nights when there is no knock at the door—nights when you learn to rely on God alone. And He comes. He comes in a verse of scripture you've never noticed before or in a line of a conference talk. He comes in a peaceful feeling after you cry through your bedtime prayers. And sometimes He comes so quietly, so subtly, you don't even notice, until one day you realize you have found healing you didn't think was possible.

I once heard a young man ask a question in a young single adult ward: "What are we not doing that we should be doing?" In response, a bishopric member's wife stood and said something to the effect of, "I know this is not true of all of you, but many of you could strive more for relationships." I knew the woman meant no harm, but I also knew what this young man was really asking: "What's wrong with me? What am I doing wrong?" I knew the question because it was the same question I had asked months earlier.

I was sitting in the Salt Lake Temple. My job during this particular half hour of my temple shift was simply to stand each time a patron walked by, and it happened to be in a spot where not a lot of people walked by. So I had a lot of time to think. And there I sat, when seemingly out of nowhere I had a feeling that my grandparents were trying to talk to me, and among other things, I "heard" these words: "You're not doing anything wrong. You're doing everything right. Just keep doing what you're doing."

So, if you currently find yourself single and trying your best with little perceived success, I hope you know that if I could, I would drop off your favorite thing on your doorstep. I would give you a big hug and tell you, "You're not doing anything wrong. You're doing everything right."

Emily Snyder

PRESIDENT OF A HOME DESIGN FIRM

———

"I prayed years ago—as I got sick and tired of praying about marriage—I was like, 'I'm sick of praying for this. I can only imagine how sick God is of hearing this same prayer. Can we shake this up?' and I prayed to know what to pray for, and how to change my prayer for that. In one of the very few times in my life, I felt like I got very clear, direct—verbiage, almost—and it was just this really weird feeling of . . . I signed up to serve, I signed up to build His kingdom, and if the most effective way for me to do that is being single, I choose to be happy being single and to find purpose in that, and trust that this is the most effective way for me to build His kingdom. That has been a prayer that I've gone back to count-less times, of: 'I signed up to serve, I signed up to build, I believe in this. I trust the God that I worship.' And so, I will build single, because I'm trusting that that is where I'm supposed to be most effective right now."

Scott Sonnenberg

EXECUTIVE FOR THE L.A. CLIPPERS

———

"Families are central to our Father in Heaven's plan, but all families are different. Some are blended families like mine, some are single mothers trying to do their best with their children, some are single fathers trying to do their best, some are a couple that can't have children, and some are the stereotypical, 'perfect' relationship with husband, wife, and kids in the home. Every family is different. So, yes, family is central to our Father in Heaven's plan, but there isn't a one-size-fits-all for families."

Sharon Eubank

FIRST COUNSELOR IN THE
RELIEF SOCIETY GENERAL PRESIDENCY

———

"I would say that I hope being single isn't the most interesting thing about us. I can remember sitting in an early meeting when we were first called as a presidency and the data was given that two-thirds of the Relief Society at any given time is single, and I just remember being blown away, because I always felt like a minority. I believe, from my own experience, there's tremendous untapped strength in the single members of the Church. Every

circumstance is going to have advantages and disadvantages too. But I want to leverage the advantages of my single period, and I don't think there's a lot of benefit in labeling us or segregating us by the current circumstance that we're in, so I really appreciate the movement of the Church right now to say, 'Life circumstance comes and goes, but our devotion to Jesus Christ, our devotion to each other, that's the most important thing about us.'"

Reyna I. Aburto

SECOND COUNSELOR IN THE
RELIEF SOCIETY GENERAL PRESIDENCY

"Our story is not over yet. . . . We need to look at ourselves in a more holistic way and with a perspective that is more eternal. We need to realize that great things are happening around us and that great things will happen also in the future. The fact that we are going through this hard time right now will give us the sensitivity and the compassion to help other people that may be going through similar situations."

Sefa Palu

PROJECT MANAGER AND PODCASTER

——

"I think I'm much more aware of His presence and I have a stronger conviction of [God's] existence because of this time of being single. I'm more aware of Him and I feel like He is more aware of me as that relationship grows stronger. There are quiet moments and there are times where the loneliness gets a bit intense, [but] . . . I'm way more aware of Him because there aren't any distractions around me. I'm in this kind of struggling time period, and I feel His presence there."

Calee Reed

RECORDING ARTIST

"My experience felt very lonely, my experience felt like God was very far away from me. And I just want to put out there that I think that there is room for all of our experiences. If you are a person who is in the boat with me where God feels very far away, I think God is teaching us through that. If you are in a different boat where it feels like God is very near you, and He is carrying you and holding you through it, what a beautiful thing. Embrace that."

Mallory Everton

SKETCH COMEDIAN

—

"I would just say that I feel that the gospel has blessed my life because it's given me a place to go. And I know that maybe doesn't sound super warm and fuzzy. But I think often about that passage where Christ asks the disciples if they're going to leave also, and they're like, 'Where else would we go?' Faith feels like that a lot of the time, where you're like, 'I don't know where else I would go.' And I feel really grateful for the gospel because it has given

me a place to go. And even when I'm not positive about absolutely every aspect of the Church or about the gospel, I have a place to go and find peace. And I think that that has been extremely valuable in my life, just to be able to go somewhere, to go to church, to go to my scriptures, to get on my knees, and be able to find peace, and find that faithful center, where I can feel like everything is going to be okay."

Sharon Eubank

FIRST COUNSELOR IN THE
RELIEF SOCIETY GENERAL PRESIDENCY

———

"I believe because God can see everything. He sees the future; He sees the past. He looks at my life, He knows who my husband is, He knows who my kids are, and He sees the line where we intersect. And I think to Him, it's an accomplished fact. So, when He looks at me, He sees the whole me. It's not that important to Him where I am on that line right now, as long as I'm heading toward His vision and the blessings that I hope I'll have. I need to think of myself more holistically. I don't want to wait around. My advice would be, take control. Take spiritual and physical control of your life. If you want something to happen, then make it happen by your faith."

Emily Snyder

PRESIDENT OF A HOME DESIGN FIRM

———

EMILY SNYDER: The heroine [in the book I was reading] was an older, single female that was desperate to get married, and had made some interesting choices along her path. And her father said, "Is it more important to you to serve Jesus Christ? Or is it more important to you to get married?" And I was livid. And I literally threw the book across the room. [I was] angry as to, why in the world are those two separate questions? That's not fair. And [that] was a deep, deep, dark day and night of wrestling with the Lord and figuring out where and how I wanted to answer that question.

MORGAN JONES: How would you answer that question now?

ES: Marriage is one of the experiences I feel like is essential to become [like] God. But it is only one of the many, many experiences for my eternal growth that is necessary for godhood. There is an eternity in which I will get to experience things, and I trust that God has a timing set for me, and for all of us, on our different journeys or paths. I don't know that I believe that God tailor-fits us per se, but I think He constantly provides opportunities. And I have complete trust that marriage is a necessary opportunity for my progressing to become as God is. And when that happens, I trust it will be when it's supposed to happen.

CHAPTER FOUR

All In
through the Tough

———

I had known Perri Correia for a couple of years when one night I received a text message asking me to read a blog post he had written. Although we don't know each other very well, Perri is someone who just has a nice spirit about him. Maybe it's the tone of his voice, but something about him puts everyone around him at ease. So you can imagine my confusion when, as I read his blog, I found myself reading a firsthand account of excommunication. (Note: *Excommunication* is no longer a term used by the Church, though it was at the time this episode was published. Being removed from the organization of the Church is now referred to as a withdrawal of membership.)

I texted Perri and tried to gain clarity. He explained that it was his first-person experience, and I said, "Wait, when did this happen?"

He replied, "Last Thursday."

As I read Perri's words and recognized his sincere determination to remain committed to the gospel, I remembered an article I had read just a few days earlier. It was written by a man who had also been excommunicated but had recently been rebaptized. And suddenly, I had a crazy idea: What if we facilitated a conversation between these two men who were on opposite ends of the excommunication process? It felt kind of radical, and I didn't even know if we *could* do it, but I did know that I didn't feel like the idea had come from me.

The end result ended up being our twentieth episode, and I will never forget the moment when Rory Mele said, "I always viewed excommunication as the justice, right? That, 'Oh, that guy got what he deserved because he got excommunicated because he

> EXCOMMUNICATION IS NOT JUSTICE. EXCOMMUNICATION IS MERCY.
>
> Rory Mele

did something wrong.' But there's more. And that's God, right? God is a God of laws, a God of justice, He can't deny His own laws. He gave us a Savior and the exercise of mercy. And now, because I've experienced it, [I know that] excommunication is not justice. Excommunication is mercy. Relieving me of my covenants that I made with Him, wiping the slate . . . clean, so that I can start fresh with new principles to lean on."

The truth is, from the very first episodes we released, we have tried to tackle tough topics: mental illness, addiction, being a gay member of the Church, abuse, and racial tensions, to name a few. I

can honestly say we have never forced our exploration of these topics and instead have waited until the right person or situation presented itself. Knowing that the Lord had guided me to Perri and Rory gave me faith that He could do it again, and He has—time and time again.

In the days and weeks after that episode with Perri and Rory, we received messages from listeners extending as far as Australia and France. I watched how the episode not only helped those who listened but gave purpose to Perri and Rory's experiences. More than anything, I have treasured my association with these two good men. They have kept me updated on their progress as they seek to regain their blessings as members of The Church of Jesus Christ of Latter-day Saints. Seeing photos of Rory dressed in a white jumpsuit at the baptism of his child brought a huge smile to my face, my eyes welled up with tears when I saw pictures of his family after their sealing, and I got chills when I received a message from Perri that said "Membership Council: October 25, Baptism: November 1, Speaking in stake conference: November 8."

YOU ARE A WITNESS TO ME THAT GOD IS GOOD.

And while the topic changes, situations similar to this have happened over and over again as the right people to speak to specific issues have presented themselves. People have come along at the right time to share their thoughts on being all in through unbelievably difficult challenges like racism, addiction, and more. To each of these people who have taken an awful chance on allowing us to tell their stories, no matter what their "tough" is, I want to say thank you for your courage and for your faith. You are an overwhelming witness to me of the good that exists in this world—you are a witness to me that God is good.

Perri Correia

BLOGGER, PHOTOGRAPHER,
HEALTH AND FITNESS ENTHUSIAST

—

"Everyone's going to have a different experience with this process. I can see where some would allow all the negative emotions that you feel to take over and push them further away from the Church—going in a different direction and just have it overwhelm them to where they don't feel God's presence in this. I think that's when we need to be more sensitive to those who are struggling with that, who may not know where to turn, or feel like they can't turn to someone. And I think, more often than not, someone who's taken the steps and made the choice to proceed with something like this, they have the faith that they can get back, but they need the help to get there. And it's hard, it's hard to ask for help. I won't ever ask anyone for help, I'm stubborn. But just imagine someone in that position. If they've taken the steps necessary to be vulnerable, to open themselves up to multiple people who they don't know—or they do know. They've suffered embarrassment, fear, and then to get the worst possible outcome, in their minds, to have that happen to them? Without support, they're not gonna make it."

Abe Mills and Stephen Jones

MEDIA PERSONALITIES

ABE MILLS: If we're looking at [it like] how can you be a member of the Church? When I tell people [I'm a Latter-day Saint], they're like, "How can you be a member of that Church? Because . . . they're racist and this and that." And I say, "You're asking the wrong question." The question isn't, "How can I be a member of this Church?" The question is, "How can people like your father, Stephen; and my father; and Darius Gray; and Elijah Abel, how could they join the  Church before Black people could hold the priesthood?" Their conviction was so strong, and their conviction and conversion were so personal with God, that they could not deny it, and could not leave the Church. They couldn't leave it because even though people will be racist in the Church, they were not converted to the people, they were converted to the gospel.

Once they became converted to the gospel—I don't want to say it didn't matter what people did, but for them, they were going to withstand what people were doing and saying because they knew what God had in store for them. I give a shout-out to those men who are real pioneers. Elijah Abel was an actual pioneer that went across the plains, but your father [Stephen], and my father, [and] Darius Gray—who was . . . [an] original leader of Genesis group—those are some real pioneers there. And I just have to give a shout-out to them because they taught me that's the question that you should be asking. How is it that those men stay faithful in the Church with all of those things going on around them? Why would they do that if it wasn't true? That's the question that you should be asking. When I ask myself the question in that way, I go, "Wow." I take my hat off to those guys, because you see what's going on now today, you say, "Well, that can't shake my faith." If what was going on then couldn't shake their faith, then what's going on now can't shake my faith.

STEPHEN JONES: You can't tell my dad that the Church isn't true. You can't.

AM: Right. Regardless of what he's seen and experienced . . . that's the way it was with my father as well.

MORGAN JONES: I just want to say something really quick before we move on to the next question, and that is, I went [to the] "Be One" celebration—I was in the Conference Center. And they started talking about some of these people—Jane Manning James, Elijah Abel—and the people stood up. There was like a standing ovation. And I just remember thinking that standing ovation was so overdue. So overdue. . . . But I also think that I know that was you, Abe, trying to say, if my dad could handle this, then I have no room to talk. But I actually do think that you do have room to talk. . . . We all grapple with different things. But to be a Black member of the Church, you have to look at the history and come to a point of believing, regardless. . . . And you may want to cast that aside, but I just think that if we all recognize that a little bit more, then that would create a space for people to feel like, "They understand that this might be a hard thing, let's talk about it. They want to listen to my experience, let's talk about it."

Corrine Stokoe

FOUNDER OF MINT ARROW

———

"I needed the Savior's Atonement as bad as any other addict who just feels like, 'I can't survive this one more day.' . . . And people ask me all the time, like, 'Well, what if Neil relapses again?' Or, 'What if he doesn't stay sober?' And I no longer feel the desperation of, 'Oh my gosh, if that happens, then we won't be happy anymore. I won't know how to feel peace.' I know exactly how to get that for myself. And that was such an eye-opening thing, doing each of the steps—that first of all there's no 'I am higher up than someone else who struggles with a different kind of addiction.' It just brings you down to the depths of humility where you really have to look at all of your imperfections and character weaknesses and things you've done wrong. And you realize that we all need the Savior equally, we're all beggars."

Lola Ogunbote

SOCCER COACH AND ADVOCATE

———

"I think everybody, Black, white, brown, yellow, whatever, everybody has a role to play. Everybody has been uniquely created to contribute. I don't think and I don't purport to know the mind of God, but I don't imagine that God wanted everyone just to be the same. I think that in His wisdom and love, He gave us things that make us unique. He loves us equally. He loves you, He loves me, He loves all of His children. Because He loves us, there's a place for us. There has to be. I just don't believe that God is a being exclusive, He is a God of inclusivity."

Laurel Christensen Day

AUTHOR AND SPEAKER

—

"We either believe that all are alike unto God, or we don't. And I feel like I spent a lot of my life being a really good member of the Church, checking off some boxes and doing this to-do list of things I thought I was supposed to do. And I think the older I get, and the more life experience I have, I'm becoming more and more aware

that really all He cares about when all is said and done is, 'Did you love my children?' And there's plenty of times I fall short of that . . . but I think a lot of us are going to be surprised by how important that question is, after this life, compared to all the other questions we thought we were going to be asked."

Michalyn Steele

BYU LAW SCHOOL PROFESSOR

"It is an expense that we have covenanted to bear—that we would mourn with those who mourn, not just hear about their pain and feel sorry about it, but do the work of mourning with those who mourn. . . . So I think it's tremendous if we can fulfill that covenant more fully, and see and hear and sit with the pain, especially of the Black community at this time that we are seeing  and hearing afresh, but they are not experiencing afresh. . . . So for us to be able to sit with that pain, not ask them to make us more comfortable in it, not ask them to just continue to do the work of bearing it mostly on their own, but truly to link arms and to shoulder the burdens in whatever way they ask us to, I think is sacred work, and it is work that the Lord would have us do as part of our covenant with the Lord for our brothers and sisters. He wants us to be one. He wants us to not just feel empathy, but to do the things that will bring some relief for those burdens."

CHAPTER FIVE

All In
Loving Those Who Leave

—

When I was serving as a missionary, I thought that the most heartbreaking thing in the world would be if one of my mission companions left the Church. I never even considered that people within my own immediate family, the closest people in the world to me, would leave the Church I thought they believed in just as much as I did. But what many people don't know is that in the time that I have hosted this podcast, members of my family have gone through several transitions of faith. In a very strange and unanticipated way, I will forever be grateful to my siblings for having the courage to explore what they actually believe. In many ways, this experience has changed me. It has changed the way I pray; it has changed my understanding of covenants; it has taught me the power of familial love and shown me just how unfailing that love is. My siblings' willingness to share their experiences with me, though sometimes painful on both ends, has opened my eyes and given me greater empathy for those who choose to step away from the only religion they have ever known.

It has even changed the questions I've asked on this podcast, as I often find myself thinking, "What would my mom want to ask this person?" or "What question would my sister want answered by this guest?"

While I wholeheartedly believe in the gospel of Jesus Christ and I am grateful that my path has never led me anywhere other than to this Church over and over again, I do believe that some have other journeys to take. It is for this reason that I will never forget Thomas Wirthlin McConkie's recollection of a conversation he had with his grandpa, Elder Joseph B. Wirthlin:

"For parents who are working with a child who's struggling and seems lost . . . let me speak to addressing the life of faith in your child and the role of the gospel.

"One of the most life-changing moments I've ever experienced came when I had been in China for a little while. . . . My hair was long and shaggy and hippie, and I'd been out of the Church about eight years. And my Granddad Wirthlin, who was in [the Quorum of the Twelve] at the time, he just called me down to his office one day to chat, real friendly like, and I was excited because I'd always had an amazing relationship with him and I was like, 'Cool, Granddad wants to hang out with me in the office. I'm there.' And I sat down across his desk that day, and he looked at me. And I'm twenty-one, the mission years [when young men typically serve] have passed. I look like a total hippie, I'm half Buddhist now. He just looked at me and just said, 'I know you're going to serve a mission.' And in my mind, I just thought, 'What does that [mean?] That's gone, that window closed.'

"And the way I make sense of that moment, now many years later, is that he wasn't looking at me anxiously as a really concerned parent would look at me and say, 'Oh, twenty-one, I think the cutoff is twenty-five, you can still get to the MTC.' He wasn't looking at me in human years. It felt like he was looking at me across the eons. . . . I believe, in that moment that was so life-changing, he was looking at me much the way God looks at His children. Because when you can only see a couple of years of your kid's life, you're going to freak out. And you have good reason to freak out if you have a kid like me at thirteen years

old, but all of a sudden, if you look at that same child across 10,000 years, and you imagine how luminous that being is going to be in 10,000 years. When you play the long game with human beings, it's like, 'Oh, their path is a little different. But wow, I can just feel the holiness in this person,' and my granddad gave me that gift. He gave me the gift of sitting across from me as a family member and not being so anxious about the next couple weeks, and he gave me a glimpse into something much bigger, and I believe God wants us all to see each other that way."

Initially, I struggled to know how to talk with my siblings. I relied heavily on prayer, frequently praying that I wouldn't say the wrong thing. With one of my sisters, I waited for the right time to say something. I did want to know what had prompted her choice, but I wanted to make sure I was in the right place to receive what she had to say. And then one night, while on a walk during our family vacation, I felt very clearly that the time was right. I waited to get the nerve up and then I just asked, "How are you doing?" What made that time right? I'm not sure, but I think part of it was just that I genuinely wanted to know how she was doing—I didn't ask with any pretense or expectation that I might change her mind.

At the end of our conversation, my sister expressed that she felt God was guiding her as she sought answers related to her faith and that she felt even closer to Him. She hoped I would trust her experience with Him. The interesting thing is that in that moment I did, and I still do now. Why? Because I have also felt my relationship with God change dramatically during the hardest days of my life. We were able to talk about how we had both come to know God over the past few years in ways we hadn't known Him before, and we each expressed gratitude for that experience. It was such a little thing but, during that conversation, I felt like we understood each other better than we had in years. We were both having our own learning moments with the same God. Sure, our experiences were taking us in different directions, but if we truly trust God, doesn't that mean we also trust the road He takes us down?

It is my belief that we all have a path, but part of being all in means that we obey the commandments—love God and love our neighbor. It means we keep our covenants, one of which is to "mourn with those that mourn; yea, and comfort those that stand in need of comfort" (Mosiah 18:9). In short, we have committed ourselves to love—to love with all we have, to let that love

> **WE HAVE COMMITTED OURSELVES TO LOVE—TO LOVE WITH ALL WE HAVE**

change and refine us, to let it break our hearts and also put them back together. As professor and writer Chad Ford told me, "A lot of people are like, 'Love, really? You're going to tell me love is going to change the world?' I'm like, first of all, from a faith perspective, love is the power that creates the universe, that is the catalyst of the Atonement, that literally changes our world. But it's not romantic love. It's not the sort of love that we hear in rock songs, or in movies. And it's not even the love that means 'like,' in that, 'I have to like you or agree with you or we have to be best friends, or that we have to have everything in common with each other.' It's not like love in that 'I love chocolate,' or 'I love pizza,' or 'I love my roommate,' or what have you. It's the love that says that your needs and wants and desires matter to me as much as my own. That I hold you sacred because you're another human being. And because of that, I'm committed to a relationship that is both beneficial to you and to me—that I'm here to help you along your life journeys, that we're in this together."

Jared Halverson

INSTITUTE TEACHER

—

"I knew their hearts before, and I know their hearts now. And their perspective on things may have changed. The perceptions they have of experiences may be different than my perceptions. But the person behind them is still the person that I loved before, and [I need] to hold out hope . . . to give them the benefit of their doubts. And to understand that the fact that they're even engaging in the wrestle is such a beautiful sign. And while their decisions right now might not be the same decisions that you would wish for them, there's something about Heavenly Father's watch care, the Father of every prodigal is still staring out the window, waiting for any movement home, and He'll run out to meet them, and hopefully, we're running right alongside them."

Patrick Mason

CHURCH HISTORIAN AND AUTHOR

—

"I think one of the things that we're called to do as Christians is to lose ourselves not only to find ourselves, but also to find other people. That this is the act of charity, this is the act of empathy, of trying to set aside our own blinders and our own preconceptions and really enter into the experience of somebody else as much as we can. We can never do it perfectly. But this is exactly what the Savior did in the Garden of Gethsemane. This is exactly what the Atonement does; [Christ] enters into our pain, He enters into our experience—our life, our sorrows, also our joys and our happiness and all those things. . . . He enters into all of those things so that He can help us. And so I think—however imperfectly—that's what we're called to do, to maybe set aside some of our own hang-ups or preconceptions or things and enter into other people's pain, other people's questions, other people's sorrows, so that we can help them."

Justin Coulson

AUTHOR AND AUSTRALIAN
GOVERNMENT CONSULTANT

—

"They are not rejecting you. They are rejecting God or they are rejecting faith or they're rejecting covenants or they're rejecting certain aspects of the gospel . . . but they're not rejecting you. And while the gospel feels like it's an intrinsic part of who I am or who we are, they still love us and they still desire closeness with us. And ironically, our guilt and our putting that guilt on them is going to be the thing that keeps them from faith more than anything. They're not going to say, 'Wow, because you've made me feel so guilty about leaving the Church, I guess I should come back.' But what might make them come back one day is the fact that they know that we love them unconditionally, even through their faith crisis or even through their faithless decisions. It's love that draws people in. It's not judgment. It's not criticism. It's not guilt and shame. It's love."

Patrick Mason

CHURCH HISTORIAN AND AUTHOR

—

"You see different models of faith . . . like Nephi. He believes as a very young man . . . the words of his father—the prophet and patriarch of the family—and he seems pretty steady throughout lots of pretty significant trials all the way through adulthood. He does, in his psalm, talk about that he struggles and that there are sins that he was wrestling with. But at least from the record, it seems like Nephi's pretty steady all the way through.

"Whereas you see somebody like Alma the Younger, who was raised in the Church also. His dad is also the prophet, just like Nephi . . . but he chooses a different path. He and the sons of Mosiah, they had incredible parents, but they chose a different path for a time and didn't just kind of stray, they were actively fighting against the Church. And it took the prayers of their parents in order to invoke the blessings of heaven to come in and intervene in their lives. And then they did a 180, and then you see the commitment of Alma and the sons of Mosiah after that.

"Everybody is going to have a different journey. . . . There are so many paths to faith, and the scriptures outline that, and maybe one thing that we can do is try to find somebody in the scriptures that sort of seems like us. And I guarantee that you can find somebody in the scriptures, whether it be in the Old Testament, New Testament, Book of Mormon, you can find somebody whose experience at least echoes yours, and see that they are all part of God's love. They're all part of God's family. There's not just one way to be a Christian."

Justin Coulson

AUTHOR AND AUSTRALIAN
GOVERNMENT CONSULTANT

———

"One of my other favorite scriptures . . . is [Doctrine and Covenants] section 123, verse 17. And this may be the most comforting scripture that I've ever read when it comes to struggling with a wayward child. This is what it says:

"'Therefore, dearly beloved brethren, let us cheerfully do all things that lie in our power; and then may we stand still, with the utmost assurance, to see the salvation of God, and for his arm to be revealed.'

"And I just love the promise. We need to do all things that lie in our power. And the reality is, what lies in our power? We need to be faithful and we need to love. . . . If we do that, if we do all things that lie in our power, we're commanded then to stand still, with the utmost assurance—oh, and by the way, we need to do that, do those things that lie within our power, cheerfully—and if we do those things cheerfully, we can stand with the utmost assurance and see the salvation of God. I just think that's an extraordinary promise. God wants our faithful, cheerful hearts. And He says, 'I'll take care of the rest.'"

Jared Halverson

INSTITUTE TEACHER

"I think too often we jump on [something] and go, 'Oh, well, what sin are you trying to hide? You don't want the Church to be true because . . .' And that doesn't do anybody any good, especially when there often is cognitive dissonance that's driving them away. Sometimes it's honest conscience on their part of, 'I can't accept a certain policy of the Church right now because my heart's too big,' and wanting to validate [that]. I've found that any chance that we have to validate those that we love—to help them see that there is goodness driving a lot of their questions, in hopes that they'll

simply put the weapons down—put the dukes down, so to speak. This isn't a fight, this is love, and we can love each other in spite of doctrinal differences, in spite of different perceptions and perspectives on the Church and its doctrine and its practices."

CHAPTER SIX

All In
Learning by Experience

———

"Ask him if he would do it again."

Do you ever have those moments with the Spirit when you get a prompting and you want to reply, "Have you lost your mind?" But that feels irreverent, so instead you try to ignore the prompting, but it persists until finally you give in. That is what happened toward the end of my interview with Josh Pack.

I met Josh in college when I was roommates with his cousin. The year was 2010, which means I never knew Josh before he was involved in an accident that left him paralyzed. It was just a simple swimmer's dive, and they still aren't entirely sure what happened, but what is clear is that Josh emerged on the surface, facedown. His brothers found him unable to breathe and hauled him back to the beach. He was life-flighted on a helicopter and woke up in a hospital bed with all kinds of tubes and monitors connected to his body.

It's not unusual for an interview question to come to my mind that I know did not come from me. But a handful of times, these questions have required that I step out of my comfort zone. Such was the case as I sat across the table from Josh. So finally I asked, "If you could go back to that day at the reservoir, would you still dive in the water?"

"That's a tough question," came his reply. "I've thought so much about it. And I would love to go back and see what my life would have been like without the wheelchair and see who I would have become without the experience. But I also know that the experience has made me who I am, [the experience] of breaking my neck and being paralyzed. There's two sides of everybody, right? There's kind of the spiritual side and then the natural man side of us. The natural man is saying, I would hit that button all day. To go back and not have to experience this and be able to walk again? That would be amazing—I would love to hit that button. But [I have] the faith to say, this is what's best for me to experience, and I'm okay to go through it, whatever it takes. And I know that Heavenly Father loves me, and through His Atonement and through the grace of Jesus Christ, it's going to be okay. I wouldn't change that for the world, to have that testimony."

I've thought about that so many times in the months since our interview—the idea of hitting a button. I've thought about the most difficult things in my life. If I could go back, would I do anything different? I think most of us would actually choose to move forward with the life we've been given, knowing what we know now, the good and the bad. Deep in our hearts, even when we feel we would give anything for things to be different, I don't think we'd press the button.

On her episode, entrepreneur Marilee Killpack recalled a moment when a button was pushed—a button that would lower her son's body down to the levels necessary for him to have a bone marrow transplant. Her son Abram, who was not even two years old at the time, had Wiskott-Aldrich syndrome, a life-threatening genetic syndrome that affects just one in 250,000 children and is symptomatic only in boys. Fortunately, his seven-year-old brother was a perfect match to donate bone marrow and save his brother's life. And yet, there was a point where doctors wondered if they should proceed. There was a question of whether or not a button should be pushed that would stop the process altogether.

"At one point in Abram's journey, when we actually started chemo, they push the button and you watch [the chemo] start infusing into his body, knowing the havoc that it's going to wreak and knowing the numbers are just going to keep going down. His levels had to get all the way to zero. And at one point when they were, I think, 200, he caught a cold. And when you don't have an immune system and you catch a cold, it's deadly. And all the doctors are coming in, they're kind of scrambling, and it was really frantic. They were trying to figure out, 'What do we do?' It was a simple rhinovirus, the common cold. They didn't know, 'Should we stop, should we wait? What do you think?' And they consulted and they talked to us about it. It was such a pivotal moment because his levels would have hit zero no matter what. And if we had waited, they would have hit zero and we would have been waiting at zero. You can't go back, there was no reversing it—that point of almost no return where we had committed to the chemo and Abram couldn't go back. He was all in. This is his shot and this was his one chance—we couldn't redo it.

"I think that moment has meant a lot to me, where we decided to just keep going forward. Where we hit the big roadblock, and you don't know how it's going to turn out, but you're already in it.

You're all in and you don't go back and you don't second-guess and you can't just stay. There's no steady, even, middle ground. You have to just march forward.

"That experience with Abram has taught me a lot about being all in. He was all in, and I'm so grateful that they didn't pause or wait, and I hope in my life I can be all in. . . . There were lots of moments where it would have been easier to just throw in the towel, but we're here on earth. This is our one shot to try it out and do it, and so being all in is diving in headfirst and embracing all that comes with that. The good and the messy and the miracles and blessings."

Isn't that what we came here for? The good, the messy, the miracles, and the blessings? All of it. We knew that it was only through experience that we could learn what we came here for, and I don't think we looked back. This was our one shot, and I think we were all in.

> ISN'T THAT WHAT WE CAME HERE FOR? THE GOOD, THE MESSY, THE MIRACLES, AND THE BLESSINGS?
>
> Marilee Kilpack

———

"This is hard for me to even believe I would ever say this: I'm so grateful for multiple sclerosis and what it's done in my life. It took me to my knees; it completely ground me to dust. And then I had to remake myself from a core and a solid belief in our eternal connectedness and in our eternal brotherhood and sisterhood, in the eternal goodness of our Father in Heaven. . . . It did give me a broken heart and a love for other people that are suffering and understanding for what that means and how hard it is because I've been there. And so I'm grateful for that. I'm really, really grateful. I say multiple sclerosis was my best teacher. It was an unwelcome teacher, but as I look back in my life now, I would never have believed I would have done what I've done or been where I've been."

Chris Williams

IBM EXECUTIVE AND SURVIVOR OF A CAR CRASH THAT
KILLED THREE FAMILY MEMBERS

———

"If there's one witness, one testimony, one concrete thing I can say I absolutely believe and know to be true, . . . [it] is that Christ loves the one. . . . Somehow, He just knew each and every one of us so individually, so perfectly, that when He went into the garden and prayed, He did it for us, for you, for everyone. Not just for a big old group, but He knew everyone individually. And for me to feel that love that He had just for that one individual, it changed everything. It changed my perspective and it's changed my life."

Leslie Huntsman Dyches

MENTAL HEALTH ADVOCATE

———

"The day after [my husband] Chad's funeral was Sunday. And I walked into sacrament meeting a few minutes late with my children and my mom, and we sat down, and they started the sacrament. . . . I was sitting in the very back, and there's that curtain that divides the wards, and I could hear the priesthood brethren behind the curtain behind me singing 'Joseph Smith's First Prayer.' I had never noticed these words before—or if I had, it went over my head—but the words that just stuck with me were, 'But undaunted, still he trusted in his Heav'nly Father's care.' That just spoke to me, like, 'Yes, you just have to trust me.'

"And so, for me to be all in, I have to put my trust in Him. I have to trust in His plan and His purpose. I have to trust in His teachings and in His timing of things. Most of all, I have to trust in His love for me, and that I won't have all the answers right now. But I do know that He loves me."

Lori Walker

—

"Sometimes, I have strangers approach me and ask me about my scars or my limp. . . . I've given a lot of thought to my appearance and how I stand out from the crowd because I don't walk as smoothly anymore, and I really am not bothered by my scars at all. At all. They don't bother me at all, even the ones that are on my face. I'm fine with it.

"I've given a lot of thought to what people say about how, after this life, we'll all be made perfect again, that we'll be whole, that everything that's been injured or harmed will be made perfect. And I consider that along with knowing that the times that Christ has appeared after His resurrection, He has appeared with His scars. He comes and shows His scars and encourages people to touch them, and He uses them to testify of who He is and what He's experienced. And I think I can learn something from that. I think that if I think of my scars as an opportunity to testify of who I am and what I believe, most especially having experienced all that we have, that's a pretty awesome gift."

Charlie Bird

FORMER BYU "COSMO THE COUGAR" MASCOT

———

"That's probably my most-asked question: 'What are you going to do?' And honestly, I don't know . . . because my life looks nothing like I originally anticipated. But as far as how I reconcile faith and [sexual] orientation, connecting with God has helped me see that my faith and my orientation are not mutually exclusive. They are both integral parts of who I am. And if I try to reject either one of those, I'm not really me. But accepting both of those, and seeing how they live together, and how they wholly occupy the same space, has given me the capacity to serve others in a very unique way.

"I think it helps me be more Christlike, and it makes me rely on the Lord, and it makes me think about how, 'You know what? I'm in this ward and I'm gay, so who can I connect with? Who needs gay Charlie in this ward? Who needs my ideas? Who can I connect with that maybe somebody else couldn't?' And I think when you take a step back, that's kind of what it's all about, right? Each of us helping one another and holding strong in the faith of Christ, who strengthens and lights and heals and uplifts us."

Spencer Hyde

AUTHOR AND PROFESSOR

———

MORGAN JONES: What would be your message, Spencer, to those who are currently struggling and who may be in the thick of mental illness?

SPENCER HYDE: You are loved. You're needed. Man, I just want to reach through this microphone and give you a hug. I remember my first day at Johns Hopkins, there was a twelve-year-old boy sitting on a bed with his head kind of dipped between his shoulders looking down at his feet. . . . I've kind of kept that image with me my whole life because I feel like that was the thing I wanted to change. And so, if you're struggling right now, just like with that boy, I want to go sit next to you and ask you your name and what's going on and how I can love you. And I hope that your neighbors are doing that too. Also, it might be a while, it might be a wait. . . . All of us are waiting for that something or that someone to come into our life and give it meaning. And it might already be there and you just don't know it yet, but keep hope.

CHAPTER SEVEN

All In
Like Peter the Apostle

———

I always love hearing my friend Rob Gardner talk about writing *Lamb of God*, an Easter oratorio about the final days of Christ's earthly ministry. I think part of it is because while Rob is incredibly talented (arguably a musical genius), I also know him to be a pretty normal guy. We've seen movies together and gone to London together, and what I appreciate about Rob is that he isn't and doesn't pretend to be someone who has it all figured out. And yet, he wrote what I consider to be a masterpiece all about the Savior of the world. He was young at the time and was enrolled in a program for film music at USC. He had been fortunate to be admitted to the program and was really enjoying it when all of a sudden, he began having ideas for what would become *Lamb of God*. He hadn't even begun writing the oratorio when he contacted the London Symphony Orchestra via email and asked if they would be willing to record his composition. They wrote back explaining cost and availability, and Gardner booked it. He then dropped out of his program at USC solely based on the good feeling he had about the project, and a few months later, it was finished. Gardner's *Lamb of God* explores the end of Christ's ministry through the eyes of those who knew Him best.

I set a goal really early on in the podcast that our focus would always be on the Savior, and I think we've succeeded. But if there is a costar of the show, it would be the Apostle Peter, who, by my count, has been referenced on eleven different episodes. As I've noticed this trend, I've found it fascinating, because what do most people think of when they think of Peter? Denial? Sinking? Perhaps one of my coworker's favorite phrases fits Peter best: "Passionate without accuracy." So how is it that a man who is often characterized by his shortcomings has also been offered up time and time again as a model of what it means to be "all in"?

I think the answer may be found in Gardner's answer to what it means to be all in the gospel of Jesus Christ.

"I'm going to answer this in maybe a bizarre way," he said. "But I would say, for me to understand what it is to be all in, we have to acknowledge that sometimes we're not."

In that one sentence I think he touches on something that is crucial to our exploration of what it means to be all in—we, like Peter, will experience peaks and valleys in terms of our commitment, our belief, and our discipleship. We, like Peter, will have moments when the Spirit of God is burning like a fire within us and other moments where our belief feels like the dimmest flicker of light, growing weaker with each passing day. There will be days when we want to share what we believe with everyone we know and times when we don't know what we believe. And I'm learning that a big piece of being all in is giving ourselves grace in the moments we don't feel all in.

As we've talked about Peter on the show, as I've studied him in *Come, Follow Me*, and as I've pondered the portrayal of him on the television series *The Chosen,* I have gravitated toward him for the same reason our podcast guests seem to relate to him: He is imperfect but he is here for it all—seemingly just happy to be there, learning as he goes.

But it's more than just that. I think we love the fact that Christ chose Peter first because if He chose someone like Peter—imperfect, passionate, sometimes even obstinate—He might also choose us. And maybe, if He didn't give up on Peter for his shortcomings, He is less likely to give up on us. We love that Peter almost always repented immediately, because how many times have we immediately recognized the error of our ways and then promised to turn it around? And although more than likely we fall short again just a little ways down the road, heaven knows we're trying—and deep in our hearts we know that has to be worth something.

Like Peter, we get really excited about the chance to follow the Savior, but then how quickly do we forget to keep our sights on Him? As musician Steven Sharp Nelson described, "I love that when the Savior was walking on the water, Peter's like, 'I want to come out to you. I can do that, I can walk on the water.' I feel like that all the time. When I feel the Spirit, I feel like I could walk right out in that water and race to the Savior with miracles in my wake. But then I experience what Peter experienced when he saw the wind and waves boisterous. And he began to sink. And he began to sink deeper. . . .

"Sometimes I think 'all in' is when Peter jumped out on the water to walk to the Savior. And I think the tremendous moment, the 'all in' moment, was when Peter was literally all in the water. And he was sinking. And I've learned that the deeper we sink, the more the upward pull that the Savior gives us, the more we will feel that upward pull of the Savior. And Peter was all in, and I have felt that too. All in, not just all in the gospel, but all in maybe even over my head, trying to be like the Savior and failing miserably. But what did Peter say in that moment? He said, 'Lord, save me.' And I think being all in the gospel is having the hope with all of our heart, striving for the faith . . . that God is all in our lives enough that when we sink, He will pull us out."

Patricia Holland once quoted the author Madeleine L'Engle, who said, "Peter was able to walk on the water until he remembered he didn't know how."[1] Sister Holland then added, "When Jesus called Peter to come to Him across the water, Peter, for one brief, glorious moment, forgot he did not know how and strode with ease across the sea. This is how we are meant to be."[2]

I've often wondered how that scene played out. Did Peter climb timidly over the edge of the boat or did he dive in headfirst? I love how basketball coach Mark Pope described it on his episode: "We love Peter in our family. We love him so much. And Peter is such an incredible example in the scriptures of trying to be all in in everything he does. When he sees the Savior walking across the water,

1. *Walking on Water* (New York: Bantam Books, 1982), 19.
2. "Joy and Spiritual Survival" (Brigham Young University devotional, January 31, 1984), speeches.byu.edu.

he doesn't sit in the boat. He's like, 'Can I come try? Will you let me come try it? Let me jump in and try.'"

I don't think any of us have any idea what we are capable of or how the Lord might be able to use us until we get out of the boat and try.

Rob Gardner continued his answer to the all in question, "Sometimes we are going to think that we're not [all in]—whatever Peter's motivations were or reasons were for denying, or whatever Thomas's feelings were, or Martha's or Mary's, in those moments, they felt like they demonstrated that they weren't all in, but they were. Their hearts were there."

I think more than likely if you're reading this book, your heart is there. So then the question is, what are you capable of if you get out of the boat? In Rob Gardner's case, he wrote an oratorio that has been performed by choirs and orchestras, inside and outside of the Church, all over the world.

What would happen if we all forgot we don't know how, if we gave ourselves grace in our efforts to be disciples, and if we simply trusted that God has a work for us to do, even in our imperfection? What if we had the faith that when we start to sink—and we likely will—He will save us every single time?

Get out of the boat, folks. It's time to go swimming.

Dallas Jenkins

CREATOR OF *THE CHOSEN*

—

"You can't fully identify with Jesus. We try to, but we're obviously not going to be perfect this side of heaven. So we find ourselves striving so hard to be perfect because He's the main character of the story that we're reading or watching. And it sometimes can result—not always, but it can result—in a feeling of just desperation, of 'I can't do this.' But when you can identify with Simon Peter and go, 'Oh my goodness, that guy who's just as bad as I am was saved and loved and cared for and poured into and shepherded by the Savior of mankind. Wow, maybe I can be loved and poured into and shepherded by the Savior of mankind.' That, I think, is a very powerful superpower to have in your walk with Christ."

Whitney Johnson

AUTHOR AND EXECUTIVE EDUCATION COACH FOR
HARVARD BUSINESS SCHOOL

—

"Peter—when the Savior wanted to wash his feet, he was like, 'No, you can't wash my feet.' And He's like, 'You have to let me wash your feet. Otherwise, you're not having any part of me.' And then [Peter's] like, 'Okay, then take my hands, wash my hands, wash my hair.' And I think they were saying, or he was saying, in that moment, 'I am willing to allow you to touch all aspects of my life, not just my Sunday life, but every part of my life.' . . . And so for me, what does it look like now on a practical basis, day to day? It's a willingness to every day figure out how am I willing to be a witness of God at all times and in all things and in all places [see Mosiah 18:9]. And so, for example, just a few weeks ago, I was doing a LinkedIn Live; it was a Sunday. There were thousands of people listening to it, and I made the choice that I was going to play 'God Be with You Till We Meet Again' on the piano. I invited people, when it was time to fast—and President Nelson had invited us to fast—I invited people who were listening all over the world to fast with us.

It's this idea of tearing down those walls. To quote Ronald Reagan, 'tearing down those walls' inside of you and me, tearing down those compartments where we try to cordon off our testimony of Jesus Christ. 'All in' is where we pull back the cords, we pull back, and we allow Him into every single part of our lives. For me, that's what 'all in' is."

Hal Boyd

PROFESSOR OF FAMILY LAW AND POLICY

"I think being all in, to me, means stumbling, making mistakes, maybe having a faltering, but learning from those experiences and using those experiences to propel us to become more like our Savior Jesus Christ. And to have a greater appreciation for the benefits of the gospel of Jesus Christ in our lives. One thinks of Peter, who had his moments of failure, of faltering, but those moments were used to crystallize a more firm foundation—were used to propel a more compelling Christian voice, even the rock upon which the kingdom would be built and led. One thinks of Paul, who was again leading the charge to persecute the followers of Christ. And yet, his experience with the divine was able to alter his life circumstances such that he would dedicate the rest of his days to preaching the gospel he once persecuted. And so I think being all in means that we're willing to recognize our fallibility and also recognize our faith and the realization that we can be made strong, that our flaws can be purified and can be refined through the gospel of Jesus Christ. And so, I hope when we feel like we're all out, rather than all in, that we can still come to a greater communion with the divine and allow that to be the fire, the fuel for our faith."

"I really think it's the idea of [being] focused on a person instead of principle. I just think when Peter and John see that man on the steps outside of the temple, and I think Peter for the first time in his life thinks, 'Man, I've watched Jesus for three years do His thing and I've stood in the shadow a little bit, in the background.' For the first time he gets to think, 'What would He do in this particular moment?' And it might be the first time that he actually gets to do that, and he says to the man, 'Look at us,' which means he's not looking at them. He's probably looking down like many of us might do in the presence of the Lord. We think, 'I would look down in guilt or shame or embarrassment,' but like Jesus, [Peter] says, 'Don't look on us, look in my eyes, I want to look at you and let you know right now you're the only one in the world.' And [Peter] says, 'Silver and gold have

I none, but that which I have, I give to you.' . . . And then the man jumps, and he starts leaping and dancing around and it's one of the coolest scenes in all of scripture, because that's what an encounter with Jesus can do. And it can happen that fast. The man had been sitting there for forty years, and one conversation involving the name of Christ, and he's a totally different person.

"But what happened to Peter before that scene, when they're on the beach, and Jesus had cooked them breakfast, and He asked [Peter] three times, 'Do you love me? Peter, do you love me?' . . . And I kind of think it's a moment where Jesus is saying, 'Yeah, I know that you love me, but I needed *you* to know that you love me, because our last interaction was one where you denied me. But even though you've made mistakes, you're okay. You still love me; we're still in relationship with each other.' . . . And Peter as a redeemed person, someone who feels loved by God, is then able to love others with that same kind of love. And to me that's what it means to be all in—to first feel loved by Him, and then go out and lift and love the way He would."

Mark Pope

BYU HEAD BASKETBALL COACH

"When the Savior is washing the Apostles' feet . . . He gets to Peter, and Peter says, 'No, you're not washing my feet, you're my master. I should be serving you.' . . . The Savior tells him, 'Well, if you don't let me wash your feet, then you're not with me.' Right? And so Peter, immediately on a dime, jumps on and he says, 'Well then, don't just wash my feet—wash my face and my head and my hands and wash everything because I want to be in, like I want to be all in.' [There are] like five other examples where he kind of messes up or it doesn't go exactly like he wants it to but then he just reroutes immediately when he learns and says, 'I want to be all in.' And I think that's what all in is. I mean, I don't think we have to look much farther than Peter to see a great example of being all in, and it has nothing to do with him living a perfect life at all."

CHAPTER EIGHT

All In
Making and Keeping Covenants

—

Neither of my grandmothers was raised a member of The Church of Jesus Christ of Latter-day Saints. My dad's mother's parents were devout Baptists and never let their daughter forget their disappointment in her decision to join the Church. I know this had to be heartbreaking for her, because her most treasured belief as a member of the Church was the knowledge that families can be together forever. And yet, in accepting that belief, she felt she had let her family of origin down.

My maternal grandmother was the daughter of tenant farmers, meaning her parents did not even have enough money to farm their own land. Her brothers were all, at varying points in their lives, alcoholics, whom she loved, and still loves, dearly. When my grandma was in high school she met my grandpa. His family wasn't wealthy, but his father had started a successful business that my grandpa eventually took over, and together, they made a life.

It wasn't perfect, but it was definitely different than the way my grandmother had been raised.

Interestingly, my grandmother's brothers all had daughters. They are good women who have raised beautiful families. No one else in my grandma's family ever joined the Church, but I've always wondered if my grandma's nieces saw in her marriage with my grandpa an example of what they were capable of having in their own homes.

At my grandfather's funeral, as my grandma's nieces came through the visitation, one after another they told my grandma how much my grandpa had meant to them. One of her nieces said, "When Lindy married you, he was like a knight in shining armor. But he didn't just save you. He saved all of us."

I believe the transformation they saw in my grandma's life—the thing that allowed them to hope for something better in their own lives—was the result of sacred covenants she had made. On her episode of *All In*, Church history and doctrine professor Barbara Morgan Gardner said, "When you look at these women, you see a power in them and an authority in them and an ability in them that is beyond their capacity. It may not be recognized by some in the world, but I think when you have eyes to see, and you're really paying attention to the influence that they're having in the world, you see a power that is coming from God that is not necessarily of their own making. I believe that that comes through the covenants that they are making and keeping with the Lord [in] their righteous lives. Power of the priesthood comes through righteousness, and when women of the Church are making and living those covenants, there's a power beyond their own that is recognizable, . . . and that comes because of their association with the Church."

It was this power that I think led my grandmother's nieces to feel as if they had been saved. As Sister Sharon Eubank recently said, "You may think your promises are just a small rowboat, but it will eventually grow to an ocean liner that can rescue hundreds of other people. Your covenants are about other people even more than they are about you."[1] There are more people than we can comprehend depending on our keeping the promises we have made with God.

This can be difficult because in many ways, covenants are a matter of playing the long game. It is certainly exciting to be baptized, to receive our endowment, or to be sealed, but these covenants—these promises—come to mean more with time. Our

---

1. Sharon Eubank, "Ensign College Devotional" (October 13, 2020), https://www .ensign.edu/sister-sharon-eubank.

reliance on them and need for them is truly discovered in the places where the rubber meets the road.

When Jon and Michelle Schmidt lost their daughter Annie in a tragic hiking accident, they clung to their covenants.

"When you feel like you are in such a desperate position [or] place—emotionally, spiritually, and physically—what do you have to hang on to? What is real, what is concrete, what is solid, what is lasting, what is enduring? What do you own, what is something real? And the thing that was the most important to us was our covenants. Our covenants bound us together, then they bound us to the Lord. And there was nothing that was going to break that," Michelle said.

When her husband was killed in Afghanistan, it was her covenants—the things she had been taught since Primary—that helped Jennie Taylor find peace.

"That's a beautiful two-way street," Jennie told me. "As I turn my life over to Him, He'll take the wheel. He'll help me. He'll lead me, guide me, walk beside me, and help me find the way [see *Hymns*, no. 304]. All of those childhood promises from our Primary days are that we will get to live with Him someday, and we don't have to wait until we die to be able to live with His Spirit in our lives. That's a promise available to us now."

I'm learning that in addition to inviting God's power, priesthood power, into our lives, covenants also give us power through perspective—power to rise above our circumstances and to achieve more than we could ever be on our own, power to overcome, and power to bless the lives of those around us in significant ways. Covenants have the power to save in more ways than one.

Jennie Taylor

GOLD STAR WIDOW

"The only way I can survive as a widowed mother of seven children with fifty years of mortality ahead of me—[that will] bring who knows what my way—is by saying, 'I'm all into the gospel of Jesus Christ.' Not because I'm great and noble; because [being all in] means I am going to access all the blessings of my covenants. I'm going to receive all that He offers to give me. I'm going to trust Him, that He knows better than I do, and I'm going to let Him work beautiful miracles out of the sorrowful tragedies of my life."

Bruce C. Hafen

EMERITUS GENERAL AUTHORITY SEVENTY

———

"We give all, He gives all, and we're all in."

Zandra Vranes

MEDIA PERSONALITY, PART OF SISTAS IN ZION

"All in for me means being where God asked me to be. And sometimes that's [a] really difficult place. When I'm all in, it also means that if I'm here, I'm also doing what He asked.... For me that 'doing' is that baptismal covenant piece, which is to bear one another's burdens, to mourn, to comfort, to take upon me His name. And so if I'm going to be here, that means that I'm here to do those things for other people. So a majority of people asked me, 'What's the best thing about your church?' And I always say, 'That it's a community that has covenanted, promised God, that they would bear my burden, comfort me, mourn with me, I would do the same to them. I didn't just promise you, I promised God that I would do that for you.' And so I'm dedicated. That's what keeping covenants is. That's the beautiful thing about my church, my gospel, my community."

Debra Theobald McClendon

CLINICAL PSYCHOLOGIST

———

"When I was a teenager, I found one of those inspirational quotes that people put in businesses with a beautiful poster, and it had this quote at the bottom of the poster. It says this: 'Commitment is what transforms a promise into a reality. It is the words that speak boldly of your intentions, and the actions that speak louder than words. It is making time when there is none, coming through time after time after time, year after year after year. Commitment is the stuff character is made of, the power to change the face of things. It is the daily triumph of integrity over skepticism.' This principle of commitment has guided my life, so when I thought about this, I thought, 'Well, what does it mean for me, to be committed—to be all in the gospel of Jesus Christ?' For me, it is to look to my Savior, and see, what *did* He do? In all things, Jesus Christ submitted His will to the Father. He yielded, even when it was very painful to do, even when it was inconvenient, even when it was not politically popular. I have been working in my life on this principle of yielding, and if we will yield, that's when I can say I am all in."

———

Marie Hafen

AUTHOR, FORMER MATRON OF THE
ST. GEORGE UTAH TEMPLE

———

"The temple is all wound up in that 'all in' . . . because Christ is all wound up in the temple. He has given us the ordinances and the covenants of the temple and made it possible, not only for us to be resurrected, but to become like Him. The temple teaches us the way He taught Adam and Eve. How do you receive the Atonement in a way that helps you become like He is?"

John Hilton III

PROFESSOR OF ANCIENT SCRIPTURE

———

"We tend to focus on the miracles like [when] Shadrach, Meshach, and Abed-nego are delivered from the fiery furnace. But Abinadi? He's put to death. Or we talk about Ammon and the sons of Mosiah and [how] they convert all the Lamanites—it's this awesome miracle. But Mormon? Mormon spends his whole life trying to convert the Nephites; they don't convert, they're all destroyed by the Lamanites, and Mormon is eventually murdered. I mean, his life does not turn out, in mortality, to have a happy ending. I think if we can shift our mentality from 'Okay, I'm going to pray and God's going to bless me with exactly what I want when I want it,' to 'I'm going to keep my covenants no matter what'—it's a powerful shift in our lives when we remember, it's okay if our kids don't do everything that we hope they will, or it's okay if I lose this great opportunity. In the long run, Jesus Christ is going to wipe away all my tears, and I can focus my hope on Him."

CHAPTER NINE

All In
Following the Prophet

—

Whether it was Becky Higgins recalling her experience in deciding to accept President Russell M. Nelson's invitation to fast from social media or Ken Alford citing President Nelson's habit of leaving a notepad by his bed in case he receives revelation in the middle of the night, I have been so touched by the guests on this podcast and their desire to follow the prophet. I have gained a greater appreciation for President Nelson's many invitations as I have listened to how these experiences changed our guests on the show.

In the case of Courtney Rich, I witnessed this change firsthand.

Don't get me wrong as you read this story. When I first met Courtney, I liked her. We were at a women's retreat, and I remember talking a decent amount with different groups of women that included Courtney. I learned she made cakes, and I tried some of them and they were delicious. But a couple of years passed before

I saw her again, and I was blown away. I will never forget feeling like there was light just radiating from her and she seemed like a completely different person. What I didn't know is that this change had begun the first time we met, with her acceptance of one of President Nelson's challenges: to read every topical guide reference under the topic "Jesus Christ." The challenge was a focus of this women's retreat, and each woman had been invited to study the verses in advance. Despite feeling that she was in a dark place due to struggles with anxiety, Courtney decided to accept.

She recalls: "I went with a lot of questions [and] a lot of self-doubt, but the challenge going into that couldn't have been more timely for me. [It] was to really get to know the Savior. . . . I took on that challenge, and I prayed at the beginning of that summer, and said, 'I will do everything you need me to do. I am giving you my all because I need this from you. I need to know that you're there. I need to know that you see me when I'm going through these moments of trial and I don't feel you, I need to know that you're there. And I need to know how to move forward with what I'm doing in life as a mother and a business.'

"I went to that conference and there were moments that I just felt like, 'Wow, every speaker is talking about butterflies and rainbows and I've never had that kind of experience.' And again, this feeling of 'Well, no one's talking about the hard stuff. Did you ever have a time that you prayed and you didn't feel like you had an answer, and you didn't feel comforted right after? Is that just me? Am I the only one?' That's how I felt there. And it wasn't until the last day, nearly the end—I can't remember what they were talking about—but it so clearly came to me: 'Courtney, there is a place for you. There's a place for everyone. We need you.' No one said that. It was just that. . . . I wrote it down in my notebook, and I just went home with this spirit of, 'Okay. I'm not perfect.' I'm so far from what I thought the ideal Church member was, but it was just that I got that answer, 'There's a place for you,' and I thought, 'Okay, I'm going to stick with this for a second.'

"Since then, because I felt that spirit so strongly and [felt] Him in that moment, it's just really helped me to realize that my relationship with the Savior is so important. . . . In the last three years, I've really tried to draw closer to my Savior. . . . In the last couple years, all of a sudden, my perspective has changed. And even though the trials haven't changed, because I'm looking more for the Savior's tender mercies each day—even if they're not related specifically to my trial and what I'm going through—in a moment of a panic attack or something, I can still know that He's there. And I can feel Him and see Him because I'm looking in a different way now."

I had no idea Courtney was struggling the first time we met, but when I saw her a couple of years later, there was no denying the transformative effect coming to know the Savior had had on her life. I was intrigued by this change, and honestly, it played a big part in my originally reaching out to her about coming on the show.

Courtney recently recalled our conversation on her podcast: "[Morgan] said, 'I saw a huge change in you, in your countenance and everything.' And I was like, 'Really? You did?' And I felt it. I knew that there was healing that I had done, and I had felt that change, but I couldn't believe [she noticed]."[1]

There is power in following the prophet, and I am grateful for a prophet who is constantly inviting us to act. I am grateful for the many people who have testified of the blessings of following his counsel or who have reminded me of his words. In her episode, Sheri Dew spoke of a question she likes to consider, "Will you go with him?"

"Going with the prophet for me means: will you heed his

---

1. Courtney Rich, interview with Bre Lasley, *Courtney: Beyond the Cake*, podcast audio, October 21, 2020.

counsel? Will you listen to what he says and pray about it, get a confirmation yourself, and then will you take action? When he says, 'I plead with you to increase your capacity to receive revelation,' will we try? When he says, 'Will you read the Book of Mormon? Will you try to be a little more careful about your social media time?,' will you do it? Will you spend more time in the temple? Will you do it? To me, that's what it means today in the twenty-first century to go with the prophet. When he declares truth—even if the truth is hard to hear—will you ponder it, think about it, weigh it, receive your own confirmation of it, rather than just lash out and say, 'Well, I don't like what he said and I don't like this and I don't like that.' Will you seriously ponder his words as though he is a prophet and then figure out, 'What will I do with it?'"

President Nelson has marked the path. He has given us clear directions. Will we go with him?

Emily Belle Freeman

AUTHOR AND COHOST OF
DON'T MISS THIS YOUTUBE SERIES

"I have felt over the past two years a stirring in my soul. I feel it so strongly, a hastening of a thought that there is an important work to be done, and it's to be done by the women of the Church. I want to be one of those women—I don't want to take that call lightly. I want to be all in, and what that looks like for me is every morning when I wake up . . . [I'm] ready to go, and the first word the Spirit whispers to me is 'Run.' Run. There's so much that needs

to be done right now. There are so many people who need to be lifted. There are so many lives that could be made better, and the Prophet has extended a call to us. I want to be part of that call. I want to be part of the gathering; I want to be part of the hastening. I want to be part of this great work."

Nathan Pacheco

CLASSICALLY TRAINED VOCALIST

———

"Whatever our talents might be, I think that it simply comes down to pretty much what President Nelson has invited us to do recently, as far as ministering is concerned. It's to truly be aware of other people and help other people according to their needs, whether you help them through music, through taking them a meal, or through just being with them, however it is that you minister to them or help them. I think that to truly consecrate ourselves and our lives to the Lord comes down to helping people, and in particular, I believe it comes down to helping people believe in themselves, because I think that one of the natural consequences of living in this life is we get beat up so many times through different experiences that I think it's very easy . . . it's like our default state to feel awful about ourselves, and so anytime anyone can breathe life back into our hearts and help us believe in ourselves, instead of doubt ourselves, I believe that that's exactly what the Savior would do if He were here. I'm positive that He would not tear us down and pick us apart."

Lori Walker

SURVIVOR OF A HOME EXPLOSION

—

"I was really excited about the challenge that the prophet issued when he asked everybody to read the Book of Mormon before the end of the year, and I accepted that challenge, but I put my own spin on it. . . . I really attached to, 'What does the Spirit feel like to you?' I became almost obsessive about the Holy Ghost and how people feel it, how people find it in their lives, how they feel guided and directed by it. I found 295 references that I found meaning-ful [about] the Holy Ghost in the Book of Mormon. I was spiritually on fire with it. I loved waking up and coming down to my office and doing my personal scripture study that I journaled along with, and I just was feeling so high on that feeling, and also feeling like somewhat of an expert on the Holy Ghost. So when it came time for me to be lying in a hospital bed, unable to participate in life much, but I could listen, I knew what I was feeling was the Holy Ghost, and it made it easy to listen to and be directed."

Barbara Morgan Gardner

PROFESSOR OF CHURCH HISTORY
AND DOCTRINE

"As we focus on God and we get to know our Savior, Jesus Christ, better, we're more and more likely to look to Them for validation. We're more likely to look to Them for how we're doing and what we should be doing; and the ideas, opinions, and processes of other people have less and less importance in our lives. I believe that that's one of the reasons why President Nelson is trying to get us to really focus on the Savior— it's one of many reasons he's trying to get us to focus on the Savior. The closer we are to Him, the less likely we are to be undermined or compare ourselves to other people."

Jacob Hess

PSYCHOLOGIST AND EXPERT ON MINDFULNESS

"It seems to me that in President Nelson asking us to worship more at home . . . he's pleading with us to receive more power, more revelation, more direct access with the Holy Spirit and with the Lord. In doing this for ourselves—which is very consistent with the practice of mindfulness—it's this idea that in the silence, in the space, there's a lot—not just in going and hearing from someone else, but for yourself."

CHAPTER TEN

All In
Hearing Him

━━━

What will we be remembered for? It's a question I think we all consider at one point in our lives, but I have to think it becomes more top-of-mind the older we get. While I can't say for certain whether ninety-six-year-old President Russell M. Nelson has asked himself this question, I do think many of us might offer similar answers if we were asked what his focus as President of the Church has been—something like "revelation," "personal revelation," or a simple hashtag: #HearHim.

During his first general conference as President of The Church of Jesus Christ of Latter-day Saints, President Nelson spoke of the importance of personal revelation. "In coming days, it will not be possible to survive spiritually without the guiding, directing, comforting, and constant influence of the Holy Ghost," he said, before later adding, "You don't have to wonder about what is true. You do not have to wonder whom you can safely trust. Through personal revelation, you can receive your own witness that the Book of Mormon is the word of God, that Joseph Smith is a prophet, and that this is the Lord's Church. Regardless of what others may say or do, no one can ever take away a witness borne to your heart and mind about what is true."[1]

That talk, "Revelation for the Church, Revelation for Our Lives," served as an introduction to President Nelson's emphasis on seeking to "Hear Him," and because it was given in April 2018, it is no surprise that when the podcast launched in October 2018, I kept noticing how often this topic of revelation came up in interviews. It wasn't always in guests' "All In" answer, and they didn't always mention President Nelson, but it was clear that this was one more way these people were trying to follow the prophet.

Elder Gerald N. Lund referred to President Nelson's emphasis as "hammering," and then quickly acknowledged that probably wasn't the right word. But he clarified, "He hits it again and again and again, and that is revelation—calling down the powers of heaven, getting on the covenant path, and gathering Israel. And without that spiritual preparation, you can have bomb shelters,

---

1. Russell M. Nelson, "Revelation for the Church, Revelation for Our Lives," *Ensign*, May 2018.

you can have enough guns to fight off a whole army, that won't matter."

THE EMPHASIS ON RECEIVING PERSONAL REVELATION FEELS EVER MORE IMPORTANT

It has become increasingly clear that all of the changes made in our prophet's first year as Church President, when it felt like he was sprinting, were inspired. And the emphasis on receiving personal revelation feels ever more important.

As explained by Chris Burkard, a world-famous nature photographer, while sharing why he is passionate about his career, "In a world that's getting louder and louder, it's never been more important to seek out the last quiet places . . . that I think the Holy Ghost could speak to us. And if we want to expect the world to kind of feel the Spirit, we have to first try and get them to a place where they can listen, and they can hear it, right? So for me, there's this kind of step-by-step process. If I can get people in nature, and I can get them to a place that is more quiet, they might be able to feel promptings or feelings of the fact that they are incredibly loved or cared about. And I think that's really what I seek out."

Likewise, author and podcaster Brooke Snow revealed that the same motivation leads her to her passion: meditation.

"[In that talk] President Nelson gave on revelation, he quotes Neal A. Maxwell saying, 'To those who have eyes to see and ears to hear, it is clear that the Father and the Son are giving away the secrets of the universe!'[2] And I love that! . . . Am I actually listening? And am I receiving the secrets of the universe? And really, the secrets of the universe that I need are, 'How do I make this work in my family?' That is my universe, it's like my own personal life, and . . . I've learned that He has so much to say if we will just create an experience, and, probably more importantly, a practice that's consistent. A consistent practice in order to receive what He's giving."

Meditation is often referred to as "practice," but gospel scholar Robert L. Millet also spoke of the importance of "practice" in recognizing revelation.

"Years ago, I went to a priesthood leadership meeting, and the visiting authorities were Elder Boyd K. Packer, Elder Russell M. Nelson, and Elder John H. Groberg of the Seventy—great three or four hours [of] magnificent teaching. In a Q&A time, one of the local

---

2. Neal A. Maxwell, "Meek and Lowly," *Ensign*, October 1986.

bishops said, 'I have a question for Elder Packer—Elder Packer, how do I come to know the difference between my thoughts and God's thoughts?' And Elder Packer gave an answer that at first shocked me a little bit. Elder Packer said, 'That is so easy.' And the guy said, 'Easy? How is it easy?' Elder Packer said, 'It's simple. You practice.' And at that point, I have to be honest and say I thought, 'That's a cop-out.' But the more I thought about it, the more I looked at my own life, I thought, acquiring the Spirit—understanding and grasping the messages the Spirit's trying to convey to you—it does take practice. It takes working in such a way that you begin to recognize eventually a voice like you would recognize any other voice."

On his episode, institute teacher Jared Halverson recalled an experience he had as a student at Vanderbilt University Divinity School. He was asked to speak to a congregation not of our faith, and one woman was very angry about our claim of being the one true Church. Halverson began to answer the woman the way he had answered similar claims as a missionary, explaining that we don't believe every other church is false; we just believe they are incomplete. He could tell by the woman's face that this was not helping his cause and found himself continuing, "And so is my church. My church is incomplete too."

Halverson remembers well what happened next. "Then I was kind of scrambling mentally, going, 'Wait, what? We've got the fullness of the gospel—what am I saying here?' And then the ninth article of faith came to mind, and I shared it with this congregation: 'We believe all that God has revealed,' across the board, wherever He might have done it, through our faith and through others as well. We believe in revelation past. Second, we believe all that He now reveals, so to talk to this group about the channel of communication that God still uses in speaking to His children. And then the third part, and we believe that God has yet to 'reveal many great and important things pertaining to the Kingdom of God.' That third part of the ninth article of faith is my favorite phrase in the articles—to see that there is yet more that God wants to teach us. And that's an admission that we're incomplete. . . . And so saying to this congregation, there are things that we don't yet know, just like there's things that the world doesn't yet know, but the difference is God has restored prophets to the earth, and that's the channel through which that additional revelation will come. To me, that has always reassured me when I face a question I can't get answered."

But President Nelson doesn't stop at receiving revelation himself. I've started to think of our prophet as a bit of a coach. In his ninety-six years of life, he has learned that the most important skill we can acquire in this life is the ability to recognize how the Lord communicates to  each of us. I actually think he is less concerned with how he will be remembered than about how we will be remembered.

As psychologist Wendy Ulrich said, "I really do believe that the Restoration is an ongoing process and that revelation is not only coming to the leadership of the Church, but to individuals that will help us expand our understanding of what our Heavenly Father and our Savior have in store for us."

It is my belief that President Nelson wants us to be remembered as a generation who knew how to receive revelation because he knows how much is at stake—he knows how much depends on our receiving that revelation. He knows this practice will lead us to victory in this life, ultimately leading us home.

Spencer McBride

HISTORIAN AND EDITOR
FOR *THE JOSEPH SMITH PAPERS*

———

"Revelation often is a process. Sometimes you're feeling the Spirit, but it's not immediately clear what you're being inspired to know or do. And that takes time. You work through your thoughts and your feelings until you come up with action or knowledge that matches up with the feelings of the Spirit that were prompting you. And I think sometimes we receive more revelation than we realize. We just are so focused on what we might call a light-switch moment where the revelation comes in, and kind of an 'aha' moment, like instantly we know what we're supposed to do. And those happen. But if we're only looking for those moments, we're missing these quieter, subtler moments. Maybe we're receiving more revelation than we knew; we just didn't know what to look for."

Carrie Skarda

PSYCHOLOGIST AND EXPERT ON MINDFULNESS

———

"One of the downsides of approaching our spiritual life and our religious faith with this sort of instant microwave mentality is that a lot of aspects of the gospel just don't work that way. You can't get personal revelation by asking Siri a question, and you can't order your testimony to be delivered by Amazon—these things, by definition, take time to grow. And we have to learn how to cultivate a patience and a stillness to allow those answers to unfold and to allow our testimonies to grow."

CHAPTER ELEVEN

All In Discipleship

———

In the middle of one of the most tumultuous times of my young life to date, I went to meet my friend Lisa O'Neil for lunch.

I was first introduced to Lisa and her husband, Scott, through another friend, Randal Wright, when I was working for the *Deseret News*. Randal told me that Scott O'Neil, the CEO of the Philadelphia 76ers, had just joined the Church after nearly twenty-one years of being married to Lisa, a lifelong Church member. As a huge sports junkie, I was all over the story and thrilled when the O'Neils agreed to be interviewed. What I didn't realize was that when the O'Neils said we should keep in touch at the end of the interview, they genuinely meant it and have made a consistent effort over the past five years to do just that. As a result, they quickly became like family.

So, when Lisa texted and said she was coming to Salt Lake City and would love to get lunch, I instantly took her up on it. I got to the restaurant in their hotel, and Lisa said, "Scott will be down in just a minute." I had no idea Scott was even in town, but a few minutes later, he sat down at our table and said, "All right, tell me what's going on." They knew I was at a crossroads in my life, so I had become a priority to them on this particular trip. For the next two hours, these two incredible people talked me through the next steps in my life.

I remember thinking how much their time was worth as I sat there, but I also knew they weren't focused on that—they were completely focused on helping me. In our podcast interview, Scott described his approach to priorities as "being where my feet are," and that afternoon, his and Lisa's feet were entirely with me.

I walked away from that lunch more confident in myself and my abilities, less afraid of what lay ahead of me, and with a better idea of what I needed to do moving forward. Sometimes I think that in our efforts to become like Christ, we forget that discipleship is really as simple as trying to be like Him, doing what He would do for the people around us. On that day, Scott and Lisa ministered to me in the purest, sweetest way, and I felt my Savior's

> DISCIPLESHIP IS REALLY AS SIMPLE AS TRYING TO BE LIKE HIM

love for me through the way they listened and through the way they showed that they believed in me.

Scott waited twenty-one years before joining the Church because he is the type of person who doesn't do anything halfway— he wanted to make sure he was all in. But on our podcast episode, he recalled a conversation he'd had more than ten years before he was baptized, when another disciple helped him see his potential. "I remember Lisa's grandmother was getting old, and she had lost her step a bit. And so, like many older people that come for Sunday dinners, what happens is they end up sitting in a chair and then nobody talks to them. And so Gram, as we called her, was sitting in a chair and I had my cool hat on. And Lisa was nudging me, 'Go talk to Gram,' and I was like, 'Why do I have to talk to Gram?' And she's like, 'Go talk to Gram.' I said, 'Okay.' So I rolled over to Grandma, I pulled up a chair, I held her hands, and I said, 'How are you doing, Gram?' We were talking a little bit and she said, 'You are going to be an incredible member of this Church.' I said, 'Oh, Gram, I'm not a member of this Church.' She said, 'You are going to be an incredible member of this Church.' I said, 'Oh, thanks, Gram.' She said, 'You are going to bring thousands of people into this Church.' I said, 'Gram, I'm Scott. I'm Lisa's husband.' And she looked me in the eyes and she says, 'You need to lead.' And I've always thought about that. . . .

". . . And I always think about that as a responsibility. . . . This Church is too small. You've got 16 million members. We've got 7.5 billion people on this planet, and we need to do more. We need to be less insular. We need be more loving. We need to be more open. We need to be more assertive. We need to leverage social media. We need to leverage the people we know, the influence we have, and we need to do a better job, because this gospel is too special, and we need to do a better job sharing it."

> ### THIS GOSPEL IS TOO SPECIAL, AND WE NEED TO DO A BETTER JOB SHARING IT.
> Scott O'Neil

All of these things are part of being disciples of Jesus Christ, but perhaps most important is what Gram did for Scott that day— she helped him see a future he couldn't even see for himself. She saw him the way God saw him.

A big part of discipleship is understanding and being confident in what we have. Interestingly, some of the most dedicated disciples I have met in my life are not members of our Church. They are women I volunteer with in a Bible study nonprofit called

Multiply Goodness. I have been blown away by their faith, their goodness, and their desire to devote their lives to God. One of these women is Nish Weiseth, who could be heard on one of our very first episodes. She spoke of her effort to be a disciple of Christ:

"There's no greater thing that you could invest your time in, that you can shape your life around, that you can build your life around, than the life and work of Jesus. . . . And so to be 'all in' means to be just that—to be transformed by Him, by His words, by His teaching, by His Spirit, and to allow that work in me to be shown to others and hopefully it would transform them as well."

Is the gospel of Jesus Christ sinking "all in"? Is it getting down deep into our bones and our bloodstream and changing our very natures? Are we coming to know Him, even the parts of Him we may be less familiar with? Are we  starting to do what He would do and to see others as He sees them? Do we feel motivated to share His goodness with others?

We will all fall short on this journey to discipleship. As musician Elaine Bradley put it, "There is such

incongruity with just being a human
and following the gospel of Jesus Christ,
because the gospel of Jesus Christ is
perfect. And we are not. Therefore, we
will always fall short—[so] I thank heaven,
literally, for Jesus, because that's the
whole point, His grace comes in where we fall short."

> ## HIS GRACE COMES IN WHERE WE FALL SHORT.
>
> Elaine Bradley

I believe it is that grace—His grace—that changes us. It makes us want to extend that grace to someone else. And we can do the same thing for each other. I want to do for other people what Scott and Lisa did for me that day in that hotel restaurant, and maybe if I am His hands for someone else, that person will also be those hands for the next person, and on and on and on.

Virginia Pearce Cowley

**AUTHOR AND FORMER COUNSELOR IN THE
YOUNG WOMEN GENERAL PRESIDENCY**

"He's allowing me to help in His work, and that
doesn't just mean Church work. That just means
rolling forth His light everywhere you go."

Ty Mansfield

MARRIAGE AND FAMILY THERAPIST

——

"About fifteen years ago . . . I had an experience [during which] I think for the first time in my life, I understood what it means to be saved. And ever since then, it's been less about being a good member, and more about being a disciple. And to be a disciple is to teach and to be in a tutoring, mentoring relationship with Christ, remembering that all things work together for good for those who love God. And so for me, to be all in means that I'm willing to be in the moment, trust the process, and believe that all things have purpose and design. Every experience that we have here is designed to lead us to sanctification, be that the mundane moments of parenting or the beautiful moments of spiritual communion, that when we do each of those, with an eye single to the glory of God, [we know] that every moment is designed to teach us something about God or to lead us into a relationship with God and living from that space."

Michalyn Steele

BYU LAW SCHOOL PROFESSOR

"We are meager instruments. We are imperfect instruments. But as we seek to use our hearts, our mights, our minds, and our strength in His service, then we're all in. We leave nothing behind. We withhold nothing from the Lord of our gifts, our energies, and He will use them for blessing His children."

Barbara Morgan Gardner

PROFESSOR OF CHURCH HISTORY AND DOCTRINE

"When we're all in, I think we're His in any way that
He wants, whether it's small or large, and anything
in between. He knows that we have committed
to give Him our all and the best of our all."

Epilogue

———

I came into this podcast with a very pop-culture idea of what it meant to be all in. On a television show, a girl tells a boy, "I am all in," and it signals commitment. When we began asking people what it meant to them to be all in the gospel of Jesus Christ, I didn't expect all of the answers to be the same. But as with most things, I have found "all in" to mean much more in real life than it means on television. All in can certainly mean someone is committed, but if we apply that meaning in a gospel context, does that signal a willingness to enter into a covenant relationship with God? And if that's the case, isn't that only the beginning? I think Jared Halverson summed this up beautifully in his answer to that final question:

"I love that you ask that question at the end of your interviews, because I hope all of us as listeners think about it every time. And am I more 'in' than I was an hour ago? What direction am

I moving in? When I was eight and got baptized, I was so excited to be baptized. I was one of those weird little kids that the gospel just meant everything to me ever since childhood, and I've never outgrown that. And I remember coming out of the water and looking up at the witnesses with my little eight-year-old face beaming—and to get the shake of the head, 'No, that one didn't count, because your foot came up.' I'm like, 'Dang it,' and so we did it again. And my dad did the prayer again, and he laid me under again, and I looked up. I tried the other witness this time instead of the one who shook his head the first, and he shook his head the second time and said, 'Nope, that one didn't count either. Your foot came up again.' And I remember just almost feeling embarrassed as a little eight-year-old, going, 'Come on, Dad, get it together. We've got to do this right.' And the third time, he made sure that I was all in. And, to me, if our baptism has to be complete immersion, then why would we think that the discipleship that follows it should be any less deep? I don't want a single piece of me poking out of the water. I want Jesus to take me all under and all in, to be buried with Him as Paul taught, so that I can be raised with Him in an entirely new life. I don't want my academic experience poking out of the water. I don't want my work experience, my life experience,

I DON'T WANT ANY PIECE OF ME NOT IMMERSED IN THE GOSPEL OF JESUS CHRIST

Jared Halverson

my family experience, I don't want any piece of me not immersed in the gospel of Jesus Christ, because it does change you. And when He raises you with Him, it is to newness of life. I am grateful for the restored gospel. It has changed me and continues to do so, which is perhaps why I spend the bulk of my time ... trying to help other people maintain that desire to stay with Jesus, to just stay in the water with Him. And if there are parts of you that are poking out, it's amazing how many times He'll patiently re-immerse us until we can finally say with Him that we're all in."

I love that thought not only because I also had to be put under the water multiple times when I was baptized but because when I was little the gospel also meant everything to me. I couldn't wait to get baptized, and I still remember seeing the temple spires the night I received my endowment and feeling the Spirit whisper, "You never planned to serve a mission, but you always wanted to go to the temple, and you made it!" But what I didn't understand as an eight-year-old or even as a twenty-three-year-old going through the temple is the depth of discipleship.

Philosophy professor Adam Miller explains: "When we talk about baptism to eight-year-olds, we always talk about baptism in terms of a kind of washing, or cleansing. But that's not the image that gets used in scriptures. . . . Baptism is meant to symbolize by way of immersion a kind of death and burial, and then we come up out of that watery grave resurrected into a new life in Christ."

Being all in begins with covenants, but that step into the font is just the beginning of our road to discipleship, and as we turn our lives over day by day to Him, we begin to truly discover what it means to be all in, and we learn why a life lived all in is a life worth living.

I love Lee Anne Pope's description of what it means to be all in. She said, "Being all in can be so hard, and it can hurt sometimes. It hurts when you give your whole heart to something and it doesn't go the way you thought. It hurts when you give your whole heart to something or someone and it ends—a mission, a career, a marriage, the life of a loved one. Being all in

> **BEING ALL IN MAKES US VULNERABLE**
>
> Lee Anne Pope

makes us vulnerable. It's a lot easier to hold back a little and not give everything and protect yourself from the pain. But when you look back on your life, the greatest moments will be the moments when you went all in."[1]

It's true. Giving our whole hearts can feel scary and uncertain, but there is one person we can trust with our hearts, and that is the person who has already gone all in for us. We have made promises with the One who will never break His promises, the One who will never break our hearts, and the One who can help us experience true joy.

Miller continues, "If you and I have a responsibility as disciples of Christ, if we have a job, our job is to experience joy in Christ. . . . The trick is to recognize the way that joy is something that arrives only when I stopped living my life for me and let it end and turn it over to Him."

President Ezra Taft Benson also spoke of turning our lives over to God: "Men and women who turn their lives over to God will discover that He can make a lot more out of their lives than they can. He can deepen their joys, expand their vision, quicken their

1.   Lee Anne Pope, "Choosing to Be All In," BYU Women's Conference address, May 2019.

minds, strengthen their muscles, lift their spirits, multiply their blessings, increase their opportunities, comfort their souls, and pour out peace."[2]

This podcast was launched at a point in my life when I was struggling to understand God's plan for me and honestly felt anger toward my Heavenly Father for disappointments and for righteous desires of my heart going seemingly unfulfilled. But despite my lack of faith, He blessed me with an opportunity to go deeper into the water than ever before. This podcast required that I study and rely on the Spirit more than ever before. And while in the beginning I felt depleted and didn't think I had much to give, I found that sometimes the "all" in all in simply means all we have to offer.

SOMETIMES THE "ALL" IN ALL IN SIMPLY MEANS ALL WE HAVE TO OFFER

Director Dallas Jenkins says, "It's not your job to feed the 5,000. It's only to provide the loaves and the fish." In many ways, this podcast has been my loaves and fish. And lately I've found myself thinking about the boy who brought all he had to offer to the Savior. Did he also eat following the miracle? I

2. Ezra Taft Benson, "Jesus Christ—Gifts and Expectations," *Ensign*, December 1988.

don't know. But in my case, the miracle of this podcast has been that God accepted my loaves and my fish and then allowed me to eat with Him.

So, like the girl on the television show, I want to say to the Lord, I am all in this relationship—for the moments of pure joy, the heartaches, and everything in between. I have made promises and covenants, and I meant them, but I will mess up. I'll get things wrong and I'll make mistakes. Still, I am committed to trying, to letting Him take me under as many times as it takes. I want to be used by Him and I want to be a little pencil in His hands. I want to jump over the edge of that boat and run to Him as far as I can before I start to sink, and when I do, I trust that He will save me. I will spend my life giving all I have to give, and in return I know that someday He will take me all in.

Now, I have just one last question for you before we wrap up. You know what's coming.

**What does it mean *to you* to be
all in the gospel of Jesus Christ?**

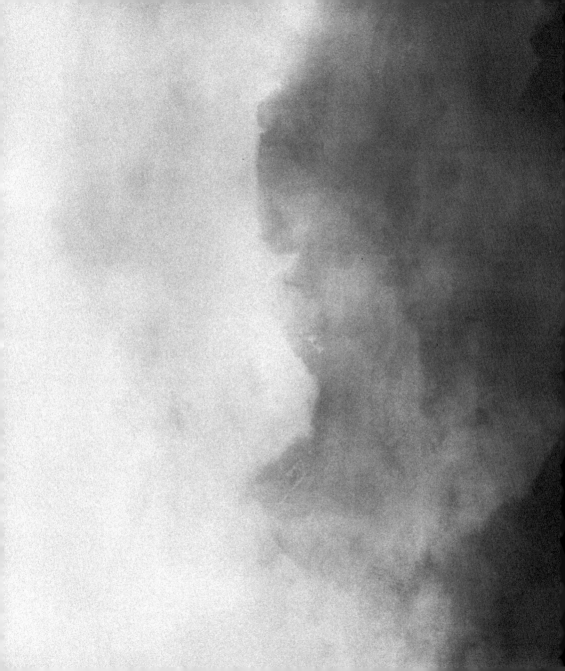

Acknowledgments

———

I would be remiss if I didn't first acknowledge the fact that this podcast has always been a team effort. I often refer to our Deseret Book audiences team as "scrappy" because the amount of brilliance that comes from a tiny little group of people continually leaves me in awe. To Erin and KaRyn, thank you for coming up with such a wonderful concept and for giving me this opportunity while supporting every single step. To Colin, Kensie, Nate, and Jake, your marketing skills took this thing to a new level, and your passion makes me want to work harder every day. To Erika, Katie, Megan, and Haley for helping with so many of the behind-the-scenes aspects of the podcast and this book. I'm grateful to you for being people I can depend on. Lindsey, Danielle, Jannalee, and Emily, thank you for being so talented with the written word (among other things) and for allowing me to devote time to the podcast. To Jasmine for creating incredible video content to complement our podcast episodes. To the rest of our little team (and those who have worked with us at any time), thank you for being a delight. Working with people like you makes my job rarely feel like work, and I'm honored to be surrounded by hearts as good as yours.

To "Derek Campbell from Mix at 6 Studios," I will never take for granted the spirit you bring with you into every interview. You are so talented, but more importantly, you are good to your core.

I am often reminded of the blessing of working for a company with so many incredible people. To Laurel Christensen Day and Celia Barnes, it meant so much to me to have the chance to learn from and work with both of you on this project. Thank you for working with me until we landed on the right concept! To Rob Johnson, thank you for advocating for *All In* from the very beginning. To Tracy Keck for bringing her gift for editing (a talent I do not have) to this book and for offering words of affirmation along the way. To Kensie Smith, you have made *All In* look good from the very beginning, and I am so grateful that you were willing to take on the design for this book. You are so talented, and I am honored that we get to share our first book! To Jack Newman and Michelle Spiron, thank you for always helping us cover our bases. And finally, to every person at Deseret Book who has stopped me in the hallways or the break room to tell me they've listened to an episode, your support has meant more than you know.

Prior to submitting this manuscript, I felt pretty inadequate to the task and tried to think of the two most avid readers I know. I then asked if they would be willing to review my manuscript. I will forever be grateful to Cristy Meiners and Jen Pearson for answering that call. They both offered their time and talents, and while I was still in their debt, they each sent me a gift when the manuscript got approved. We all need friends like that.

I am so thankful for parents who have served as my teachers and editors since I was a little girl. They instilled in me a love for writing and a passion for people and their stories, and they have always pushed me to be better. To my siblings, I love you more than words can say and am so proud to be your big sister.

To Benjamin, I love you. Thank you for making me feel like I can do anything and thank you for sliding into my DMs.

A huge thank you to every guest we have ever had on the show. While this book includes only a portion of our guests, each person has brought with them a spirit and a perspective that I have been so grateful to learn from. Thank you for taking a chance on us and trusting me with your story.

Finally, to my Heavenly Father, I give thanks for allowing me a chance I could've never even dreamed up. As Elizabeth Barrett Browning wrote in her *Sonnets from the Portuguese 26,* "God's gifts put man's best dreams to shame." This has certainly been the case for me.

Contributors

—

REYNA ISABEL ABURTO was born in Nicaragua. She has worked in the language industry for more than twenty-five years and owns a small translation business with her husband. She served on the Primary General Board from 2012 to 2016 before becoming a counselor in the Relief Society General Presidency.

CALEE REED ADAMS has released four albums through Shadow Mountain Records. Her most recent album, *Take Courage My Heart*, was released in October 2020. Her music has been greatly influenced by life experiences including losing her mother to cancer in 2011 and her own divorce and remarriage.

CHARLIE BIRD was Cosmo the Cougar, Brigham Young University's beloved mascot, from 2016 to 2018, and received national acclaim for his multiple dance performances with the BYU Cougarettes. He is the author of *Without the Mask*.

HAL R. BOYD is an associate professor of family law and policy in Brigham Young University's School of Family Life. He previously ran the opinion pages at the *Deseret News* and has written articles and essays for numerous venues, including *The Atlantic*, *The National Review*, and *The Weekly Standard*.

ELAINE BRADLEY is best known as the drummer for the rock band Neon Trees, but she is also in another band called Noble Bodies. Most recently, she has worked as the host of BYUtv's *Grace Notes*. She currently resides with her husband and children in Germany.

Photographer **CHRIS BURKARD** is an accomplished explorer, photographer, creative director, speaker, and author. His visionary perspective has earned him opportunities to work on global prominent campaigns with Fortune 500 clients, appear as a TED speaker, develop specialty product lines, teach national and international photography workshops, and publish a collection of books.

DAVID BUTLER cohosts the popular YouTube scripture study channel *Don't Miss This* with Emily Belle Freeman and is the author of many religious books, including *Almighty*, *Redeemer*, and *Spirit*.

OLGA CAMPORA was raised in Czechoslovakia under Communist rule. She is the author of *Saint behind Enemy Lines*, which details her incredible conversion to The Church of Jesus Christ of Latter-day Saints.

PERRI CORREIA grew up on the island of Oahu and has a passion for health and fitness. He maintains a faith-based blog and enjoys traveling as he develops his hobby of landscape and fashion photography.

JUSTIN COULSON has written six books and is a four-time best-selling author. He is an occasional contributor for the *New York Times* and appears regularly in all of Australia's major news outlets for television, radio, and print. He is a TEDx speaker and has also served as a consultant to the Australian government's Raising Children Network.

LAUREL CHRISTENSEN DAY is the President of Deseret Book. She previously worked for Deseret Book as the director of entertainment, the director of Time Out for Women, and the Vice President of Product.

SHERI DEW has authored several books, including the biographies of Ezra Taft Benson and Gordon B. Hinckley. Her most recent book is titled *Insights from a Prophet's Life: Russell M. Nelson*. She served as Second Counselor in the General Presidency of the Relief Society from 1997 to 2002. She is currently the executive vice-president and chief content officer at Deseret Management Corporation.

ERIC DYCHES is the cofounder of the Emily Effect, a movement and initiative named in honor of his late wife, Emily Cook Dyches, who suffered from and later succumbed to a debilitating postpartum mood disorder. The Emily Effect seeks to provide resources to families and support for women suffering from perinatal mood disorders.

LESLIE HUNTSMAN DYCHES lost her first husband, Chad, to a fourteen-year battle with depression. She is now married to Eric Dyches. Together, they are raising their collective eight children and seeking to honor the memory of their late spouses by speaking out about mental health.

While serving as the First Counselor in the Relief Society General Presidency, **SHARON EUBANK** is also employed as the director of Latter-day Saint Charities. A native of Redding, California, she taught English as a second language in Japan, worked as a legislative aide in the US Senate, and owned a retail education store in Provo, Utah, prior to becoming employed by the Church's Welfare Department in 1998.

MALLORY EVERTON gained recognition as part of the original cast of the wildly popular BYUtv sketch comedy show *Studio C*. Along with her fellow original cast members, she is now working to develop and create content for JK Studios, a family-friendly comedy network.

CHAD FORD'S name is most likely recognized for his work as a basketball analyst and writer at ESPN, but his true passion is conflict mediation and peace-building. Today, he is a professor at BYU–Hawaii as well as a senior consultant and facilitator for the Arbinger Institute. His new book, *Dangerous Love*, weaves Ford's diverse experiences into a deeply personal exploration of how we transform fear and conflict.

EMILY BELLE FREEMAN is a best-selling author and favorite speaker at Time Out for Women. She is also the cohost of *Don't Miss This*, a scripture study channel on YouTube, as well as the cofounder of Multiply Goodness, an interfaith nonprofit seeking to build bridges through Bible study.

BARBARA MORGAN GARDNER is an associate professor of Church history and doctrine at Brigham Young University. She is the author of *The Priesthood Power of Women* and a moderator for BYUtv's *Come Follow Up*.

ROB GARDNER is perhaps best recognized as the composer of the sacred music oratorios *Joseph Smith the Prophet* and *Lamb of God*. He also arranged the version of "Savior, Redeemer of my Soul" that has become a Latter-day Saint favorite.

BRUCE C. HAFEN was called to the First Quorum of the Seventy in 1996 and has been a General Authority Emeritus since 2010. An internationally recognized family law scholar, he has served as president of BYU-Idaho, dean of the BYU Law School, and provost at BYU.

MARIE K. HAFEN has taught at BYU-Idaho, the University of Utah, and BYU-Provo—classes in Shakespeare, writing, and the Book of Mormon. She has been a contributing author to several books in addition to serving on the Young Women General Board, on the

Deseret News board of directors, and as matron of the St. George Utah Temple.

Prior to his current assignment at the Salt Lake Institute, **JARED HALVERSON** spent eight years directing the seminary and institute programs in Nashville, Tennessee. He is currently completing a doctorate in American religious history focusing on anti-religious rhetoric. He currently hosts a verse-by-verse *Come, Follow Me* study on YouTube called *Unshaken*.

JACOB HESS served on the board of the National Coalition of Dialogue and Deliberation and is Executive Director of the Council for Sustainable Healing. He has a PhD in clinical-community psychology from the University of Illinois, Urbana-Champaign. He co-authored *The Power of Stillness: Mindful Living for Latter-day Saints*.

CHELSIE HIGHTOWER is best known for appearing on *So You Think You Can Dance* and as a professional dancer for seven seasons of *Dancing with the Stars*. The Emmy-nominated choreographer is now the founder of Inside Out and Dance Elevated, companies that seek to help dancers focus on developing as human beings while also striving to become better dancers.

JOHN HILTON III is an associate professor of ancient scripture at Brigham Young University. Prior to his position at BYU, he worked with seminaries and institute programs of The Church of Jesus Christ of Latter-day Saints in a variety of capacities. He is the author of multiple books, including *The Founder of Our Peace.*

SPENCER HYDE is the author of *Waiting for Fitz*, a fictional book based on his real-life experiences with obsessive-compulsive disorder. He is currently an English professor at Brigham Young University.

DALLAS JENKINS is the son of celebrated *Left Behind* author Jerry Jenkins, but Dallas has made a name for himself as writer and director of *The Chosen*, the incredibly successful multi-season series about Jesus Christ.

JANIECE JOHNSON specializes in American religious history—specifically Mormon history, gender, and the prosecution for the Mountain Meadows Massacre. Dr. Johnson has graduate degrees in American history and theology from Brigham Young University, Vanderbilt's Divinity School, and the University of Leicester in England.

WHITNEY JOHNSON is an executive education coach for Harvard Business School and the author of multiple books, including *Disrupt Yourself*. She cofounded the investment fund Rose Park Advisors with Clayton Christensen. In 2018, she was named a Top Voice by LinkedIn, and in 2019, she was number 14 on the Thinkers50 list. She is the host of the *Disrupt Yourself* podcast.

STEPHEN JONES is a native of Tallahassee, Florida. He is a comedian and actor who is perhaps best recognized for his role in the iconic BYU library parody of an Old Spice commercial, which has been viewed more than 3.5 million times on YouTube. Today, Jones is a seminary teacher.

In 2014, following a successful Kickstarter campaign, **MARILEE KILLPACK** cofounded Gathre, a modern leather goods company that seeks to make space for the worthwhile. Gathre has since expanded its product line, but its original mats have been featured by *Vogue*, *Reader's Digest*, and *New York Magazine*.

McARTHUR KRISHNA comes from a pack of storytellers. She co-owned Free Range, an award-winning marketing business focused on telling social justice stories. After she moved to the magical land of India, she got married and started writing books and raising kids.

After surviving an attempted murder, **BRE LASLEY** founded Fight Like Girls to raise awareness that self-defense is a mental, emotional, and spiritual effort as well as physical. She recently launched the Bia Movement, which provides holistic resources to disrupt the conversation, approach, and practice of self-defense.

GERALD N. LUND served for thirty-five years in the Church Educational System and was a member of the Second Quorum of the Seventy from 2002 to 2008. He is the best-selling author of both fiction and nonfiction and is perhaps best known for his historical novels.

TY MANSFIELD is a practicing marriage and family therapist and an adjunct professor at Brigham Young University. Ty has actively practiced mindfulness for over ten years and is one of the authors of *The Power of Stillness: Mindful Living for Latter-day Saints.*

PATRICK MASON is the Leonard J. Arrington Chair of Mormon History at Utah State University. He has addressed Latter-day Saint culture and doctrine in media outlets, including the *New York*

Times, Los Angeles Times, Washington Post, Chicago Tribune, ABC News, NPR, and PBS.

SPENCER W. McBRIDE is a historian and documentary editor at The Joseph Smith Papers and the host of The First Vision podcast. He is also the author of Pulpit and Nation: Clergymen and the Politics of Revolutionary America.

DEBRA THEOBALD McCLENDON is a licensed psychologist in the state of Utah. She is a clinical psychologist with training in marriage and family therapy. She focuses her practice on helping those with religious OCD, or scrupulosity.

THOMAS WIRTHLIN McCONKIE has been a mindfulness teacher and practitioner of more than twenty years, as well as a researcher in the field of adult development. He is the author of Navigating Mormon Faith Crisis.

RORY MELE is a husband, a father to three, and an advocate for an infant daughter with Down syndrome, congenital heart defects, and other medical complexities, as well as for a son with Crohn's disease. He gained a love of writing as a public affairs officer for the U.S. Army, and a love for the plain and simple doctrines of the Church through enduring hard things.

ADAM S. MILLER is a professor of philosophy at Collin College in McKinney, Texas. He is the author of many books, including *Letters to a Young Mormon*, *Future Mormon: Essays in Mormon Theology*, *Grace Is Not God's Backup Plan*, and *The Gospel According to David Foster Wallace*.

ROBERT MILLET is the former dean of religious education at Brigham Young University. He is a professor emeritus of ancient scripture, and he is the author of many books, including *The Holy Spirit: His Identity, Mission, and Ministry* and *I Saw a Pillar of Light: Sacred Saving Truths from Joseph Smith's First Vision*.

ABE MILLS was a member of Jericho Road, a singing group that performed Christian music. These days, you can join over half a million people in following Abe and his family on their YouTube channel, *Sunshine Mafia*.

As a member of the Piano Guys, **STEVEN SHARP NELSON** has nearly 7 million followers on YouTube. Steven's albums with the Piano Guys have gone gold and platinum in six countries and have held the number-one spot on multiple Billboard charts. He has performed on *The Tonight Show*, *TODAY*, *Good Morning America*, and *The Katie Couric Show*.

LOLA OGUNBOTE was born in Nigeria but raised in London, England. She has a law degree and was a practicing barrister before giving it all up to become a youth soccer coach for Arsenal Football Club within its community football department. She is now the head of soccer at Beijing Royal School, coaching their U16 and U18 teams.

SCOTT O'NEIL is the CEO of the NBA's Philadelphia 76ers. Prior to joining the Sixers, O'Neil served as president of Madison Square Garden Sports and senior vice president of the NBA. He joined the Church in 2016 after being married to his wife, Lisa, a lifelong member of the Church, for nearly twenty-one years.

EMILY ORTON is a former English teacher turned homeschooling mom. She and her husband, Erik, are the co-authors of a book titled *Seven at Sea*, about their family's experience living on a boat.

A classically trained tenor, **NATHAN PACHECO** has performed all over the world, including touring the United States, Canada, and

Mexico with Yanni. In 2017, Nathan released his first spiritual album, *Higher*, which was followed by *My Prayer* in 2019.

JOSH PACK is a CPA who currently works as a controller at Risas Dental and Braces. He graduated from Weber State University, earning both a bachelor's degree and a master's degree.

A native of Australia, **SEFA PALU** graduated from Brigham Young University–Idaho. By day, he is a project manager in the home care sector. By night, he creates content for his podcast, *Nights at the Brown Table*.

VIRGINIA PEARCE COWLEY is the author of the best-selling book *A Heart Like His: Making Space for God's Love in Your Life*, and has edited and co-authored several additional books, including *Glimpses into the Life and Heart of Marjorie Pay Hinckley*. She has served as a counselor in the Young Women General Presidency and on the Primary General Board of The Church of Jesus Christ of Latter-day Saints.

The daughter of a coach before becoming the wife of a coach, **LEE ANNE POPE** worked for ESPN prior to spending four years as David Letterman's personal assistant.

MARK POPE played professional basketball for nine years before working as an assistant coach at Wake Forest University. He became the head coach at Brigham Young University after four seasons as head coach at Utah Valley University.

JENNY REEDER is a nineteenth-century women's history specialist for the LDS Church History Department. She has a PhD in American history from George Mason University, with an emphasis in women's history, religious history, memory, and material culture.

Prior to starting *Cake by Courtney*, **COURTNEY RICH** received a bachelor of arts degree from Brigham Young University in broadcast journalism. She has combined her cake-baking expertise with her education to create a wildly popular Instagram account. She has been featured on *Oprah Magazine*, *TODAY*, and *The Kelly Clarkson Show*.

Originally from Richmond, Virginia, **LINDSAY RICKS** graduated from Brigham Young University in public relations and business. She served a mission in Santiago, Chile, before working as an event planner in Washington, D.C.

ANN ROMNEY is the two-time best-selling author of *The Romney Family Table* and *In This Together*. She is also the Global Ambassador for the Ann Romney Center for Neurologic Diseases at Brigham and Women's Hospital. In 1998, she was diagnosed with multiple sclerosis. She has volunteered much of her time to raise awareness of the disease.

MICHELLE SCHMIDT is the mother of Annie Schmidt, who passed away in a hiking accident in Oregon in the fall of 2016. Michelle is married to Jon Schmidt, of the Piano Guys.

CARRIE L. SKARDA is a psychologist who has provided individual and couples therapy with particular interest in attachment trauma and mindfulness for the last 18 years. She is one of the co-authors of *The Power of Stillness: Mindful Living for Latter-day Saints*.

RYAN SMITH is the CEO and cofounder of Qualtrics. In October 2020, Smith and his wife, Ashley, purchased the Utah Jazz from fellow Latter-day Saint Gail Miller and family.

BROOKE SNOW is a published author, podcaster, educator, and speaker. Her online courses seek to help bridge the gap between self-help and the gospel. Most recently, she collaborated on the Small Seed Still app.

EMILY SNYDER is the former chief of staff for Magnolia, the company owned by Chip and Joanna Gaines of *Fixer Upper* fame. She previously worked as executive assistant for Clayton Christensen and is now president of Establish Design LLC.

SCOTT SONNENBERG is the Chief Global Partnerships Officer for the LA Clippers. Previously an executive with the Chicago Bulls, Scott has nearly twenty years of experience in prospecting, negotiating, and closing partnerships across the globe with some of the largest companies in the world.

MICHALYN STEELE, a professor at the BYU Law School, began her legal career with a highly regarded D.C. firm specializing in the representation of Indian tribes before working for six years as a trial attorney in the U.S. Department of Justice's Civil Rights Division.

In 2018, **CORRINE STOKOE** and her husband, Neil, who are best-known for their blog and brand Mint Arrow, opened up about another large part of their family's life: finding healing, hope, and recovery from pornography addiction. The success of Mint Arrow has been featured by *Forbes*, *Business Insider*, *Adweek*, and *Allure*.

JENNIE TAYLOR is a gold-star widow from North Ogden, Utah. Her husband, Major Brent Taylor, was killed in Afghanistan in 2018. She is the mother of seven children, and, in 2020, she was sworn in as the civilian aide to the Secretary of the Army for the state of Utah.

WENDY ULRICH is the former president of the Association of Mormon Counselors and Psychotherapists. She has been a visiting professor at Brigham Young University and serves as an advisor on mental health for missionaries for the Church. She has authored multiple books, including *Live Up to Our Privileges*.

ZANDRA VRANES is a popular multimedia personality and one of the Sistas in Zion. Along with Tamu Smith, she focuses on humorous aspects of faith and Mormon culture, seeking to uplift, inspire, bridge religious divides, and create healthy dialogue.

LORI WALKER is a wife, mother, and beloved contributor in her community. In February 2019, Walker survived an accidental home explosion—a miracle she attributes to courage and kindness.

NISH WEISETH is the cofounder of Multiply Goodness, an inter-faith nonprofit seeking to build bridges through Bible study. She is also an author whose op-ed pieces have been published in *Cosmopolitan*, *Christianity Today*, and the *Deseret News*.

In January 2014, **KIM WHITE** was fourteen weeks pregnant with her second child when an eleven-centimeter tumor was found in her right adrenal gland. During her six-year battle with cancer, Kim White inspired thousands through her Instagram account, @kimcankickit.

CHRIS WILLIAMS began his career as an IT architect and systems engineer. He is now an executive with IBM. After the death of his wife Michelle and two of their four children, he married Mikkel Fuhriman Jones, a widow with two young children.

CAMRON WRIGHT has a master's degree in writing and public relations. He is the author of several acclaimed novels, including *Letters for Emily*, *The Rent Collector*, *The Orphan Keeper*, and *In Times of Rain and War*.

9/11 - Morgan Jones talk - Syracuse
1. Contention: this is a choice. How to avoid
contention. 1). Contention is not new.
2) All through scriptures - Contention should
be avoided at all costs. 3). The world overflows
with contention. How do we avoid contention
(Can't control others volume of contention, but can
control our response.) 3). The source of contention,
and the one who wants it is Satan. 4). When
contention is here, the Lord leaves.
4). If you feel Satan is pounding on you
He works to drive a wedge between us and our
relationships. - marriage? Don't want a contentious
home
   1). pray to have the love of God in your heart
   2). learn to control your tongue
   3). don't allow emotions take over.
   4). don't let the same issues
   5). speak in calm softvoice
   how you treat someone when you first see
   them will determine how the rest of the day will go.
   the Savior can heal hurt feelings.
   - What do we give the people we love the
     most - the burnt cookies or the
     beautiful ones that were meant for the
     party.
   ~ In places outside our home we the
     chances to be kind to others. If
     someone is rude to you - be kind.
   ~ Pray for what people need. He will tell you.

What does it mean to you to be *all in*?

—